KU-666-553

2245638

RIO DE JANEIRO THE COOKBOOK

LETICIA MOREINOS SCHWARTZ

Food Photography by Kate Sears

K

First published in Great Britain in 2013
by Kyle Books
67-69 Whitfield Street
London W1T 4HF
www.kylebooks.com

ISBN: 978-0-85783-208-5

Project editor Anja Schmidt
Designer Two Associates
Food Photographer Kate Sears
Food styling Paul Grimes
Prop styling PJ Mehaffey
Copy editor Leda Scheintaub
Production by Nic Jones and David Hearn

A Cataloguing in Publication record for this title is available from the British Library

Colour reproduction by ALTA London
Printed and bound in China

AMOR CIGANO
COCO
REFRI
MATTE
GATORADE
AGUA
CERVEJA
BATATA FRITA
CALABRESA
MOCOTO
HAMBURGER
MISTO QUENTE
PEIXES
SARDINHA
FLAVOUR
COCO 250
Carioca como você.
Nestlé

INTRODUCTION

I am horrible with dates, but one date I don't ever forget is 17 February 1997, the day I moved to New York to study culinary arts and devote my life to cooking. I am usually very emotional, and looking back at that date, I am surprised at my big smile while my family was bursting into tears at the airport farewell. In retrospect, I knew that day that this book was somewhere in my future – and the reason for my big smile.

It took me over a decade to turn my passion for cooking into a career. I went to cooking school, worked in restaurants and studied food journalism, and soon enough I was the proud author of *The Brazilian Kitchen*, my first cookbook.

After the book came out, I started my blog, chefleticia.com, which documents my discoveries around Brazil. With blogging, I integrated writing and photography into my cooking life. While I am not a professional photographer, I took many of the photos featured in this book.

Throughout my travels (though there is so much I still have to see!), I began to realise that my love for Brazil is as big as the country – but my heart belongs to Rio de Janeiro. I also realised that my life was shaped by the foods in Rio, and that much of what I do today is linked to something in Rio. From the juices I drink every morning, like Brazilian-style Limeade (page 34) and the sandwiches I eat for lunch, like Chicken Salad with Carrots and Chives on Wholemeal (page 134), to the foods I serve at my kids' birthday parties, like Brigadeiro (page 27) – it's all about Rio.

FINDING RIO'S CULINARY HEART

When I set out to write this book, I wanted to bring the cuisines of Rio to the same popular level as our other assets: the beach, music, samba, Carnival and football. This meant getting to the heart of Rio's most talented people and discovering the most delicious recipes.

I met some incredible chefs like Kátia Barbosa from Aconchego Carioca, Portuguese cooks like Manuela Arraes, home cooks like Ivani de Souza Ferreira and many more, all of whom you'll find here in this book. I was amazed by their knowledge, their simple approach to cooking and the wonder of their recipes.

I am fascinated by Brazilian culture: we are a mixture of African, Portuguese and native Indian influences – and we are proud of our origins. This mixture can be seen in the music we hear, in the foods that we eat and in the faces of our people. In different parts of the country, however, you will find one dominant influence over the others. And in Rio, my friend, it tastes like Portugal. The cooking of Rio is dominated by the lusitanic flavours of salt cod, onions, garlic, bay leaves and egg yolk pastries – flavours that are bright and alive in the pages of this book.

I go back home at least twice a year with my kids, and we spend a good chunk of time in Rio (though never enough), especially during the summer. I explore my hometown with the eyes of a hungry carioca woman who misses home. I take my kids all over Rio, and we go on frequent trips to the outskirts of Rio, like Búzios, Paraty, Teresópolis and Petrópolis – neighbourhoods included in this book. As I explored the city with a new perspective, I came to discover a Rio completely different from the one I left.

When I left for America, the food culture in Rio was nothing compared to the magnitude of today's trends. At that time, Confeitaria Colombo at Centro was one of the biggest bakeries in Rio. And their ham and cheese

folheado (page 120) remain my favourite! Today, however, you'll find modern bakeries specialising in different treats like cupcakes, macarons and chocolates. The only English you'd hear in the '90s was from tourists, while today there are people from all over the world living and working in Rio.

Brazil is changing, and Rio is changing with it. Over the past decade, my hometown has boomed, restoring itself to the global stage as a portal for two huge world events: the World Cup in Spring 2014 and the Olympics two years later.

Not coincidently, dining in Rio gets better all the time. Many new restaurants are opening, and Rio is becoming quite a culinary contender. Rio doesn't aspire to be fancy, but we do aspire to eat delicious, amazing food that is as casual as our city, and that is the kind of food you'll find in this book: simple and delicious.

Choosing the recipes was the hardest part. What you see here is only a highlight of Rio's best, but if you visit me in my Rio or Connecticut, USA kitchen, these are the recipes I would prepare for dinner.

Rio is my foundation; it defines me as a person. I think of all the foods I ate at home growing up like Baked Rice with Chicken and Chorizo (page 189) or my aunt's Moroccan Meatballs (page 182), and the memories of my home in Rio come alive. That's why I've also included a chapter on home cooking. These recipes are not only part of my memories, they are part of cariocas' daily lives.

MARINA

THE NEIGHBOURHOODS

Rio is a very easy city to navigate with the beach as a point of reference. That's why I structured this book by location: each neighbourhood with its own personality and my favourite recipes from each.

I focused mostly on the neighbourhoods of Zona Sul because that's where I grew up and where the famous neighbourhoods like Ipanema, Copacabana and Leblon are located. It's also where I hunt for recipes and discoveries. But that doesn't mean you should drink a caipirinha only at the Academia da Cachaça (page 16), or eat *rissoles de camarão* (page 18) only at Jobi. On the contrary, you can eat out constantly in Rio, and most of the recipes in this book can be found pretty much all over town, way beyond Zona Sul. Be aware though that, as in any metropolitan city, things change fast, with places opening and closing and restaurants changing addresses and opening other branches. It happens all the time in Rio!

Most of the restaurants featured in this book have been in business for a steady chunk of time, like Terzetto, Olympe, Antiquarius, Jobi and many others – and I include addresses and websites, when available, for every restaurant mentioned in this book. I am sure by the time this book comes out, however, even more new restaurants will be opening (enticing me with a taste for more!).

My hope is that these recipes can serve as a guide for you to understand the culinary dynamics of Rio, but most importantly that your own cooking will blossom with the use of this book.

I love the rhythm of Rio, the passion, the electricity, the music and, most importantly, the way people cook. The incredibly talented people featured in this book are making Rio a very special place to eat today. Unquestionably, Rio is a global tourist destination. I hope this book proves that Rio is not just about the carnival, beach, football and music. It's about the food as well. And I hope that this book will endure past the upcoming big events – as the recipes are as timeless as the city itself.

1

LEBLON

THE SPIRIT OF BOTEQUIMS

A *botequim* is a simple type of restaurant that came into being in Brazil in the late 1800s by and for Portuguese immigrants – a place where they could meet, unwind, eat *petiscos* (finger food) and drink, but mostly to take a break from home and work.

The staff typically consists of veteran Portuguese waiters who often have been in the business for just about their whole lives. Today they are as much a part of the scene as the food. The menus are usually written on chalkboards, the tables are squeaky and the chairs are bare. But the atmosphere is mystical. Ideas, conversations, friendship and music tend to flow through the tables of botequims in a way unlike anywhere else.

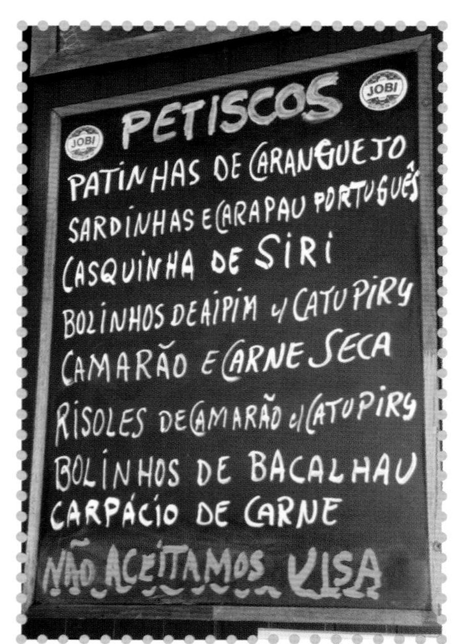

You see people in their twenties, in their eighties and everyone in between, but most of the regulars who gravitate towards botequims are artists and musicians.

'The Girl from Ipanema' was written by Vinícius de Moraes and Antônio Carlos Jobim while the two were sitting at a botequim in Ipanema at the corners of Prudente de Moraes and Vinícious de Moraes streets enjoying their caipirinhas. Like the girl from Ipanema, whose walk is more than a swing, a botequim is more than a restaurant. The melody in your mind can be happy or sad; whatever mood you're in, the botequim is likely to soothe your soul.

Perhaps the most noteworthy virtue of a botequim is that it is an extension of the beach, bringing people together beyond differences of class, race and occupation.

I cannot think of Rio without botequims. They are part of our culture and part of our spirit. And no matter how trendy we aspire to be, how vogue the food culture becomes, the botequim is the essential bridge between past and present, nature and culture, food and music, and Portuguese influence and Brazilian habits.

JOBI
JOBI

Caipirinha
SUGAR AND LIME COCKTAIL

RESTAURANT: Academia da Cachaça,
R. Conde Bernadotte, 26 – Leblon,
academiadacachaca.com.br

Of all things Brazilian, you've probably heard of the caipirinha, our heraldic emblem and one of Brazil's greatest contributions to the food and wine world. The spirit behind it, cachaça, was invented in the mid-1500s in Brazil when Portuguese colonisers began to cultivate sugar cane. Somewhere in a sugar mill around São Paulo, some stems of rough sugar cane were forgotten, left to sit around and fermented into a foamy juice. The drink, though non-alcoholic, had a strong effect on the body and was used as a painkiller.

Eventually the Portuguese decided to distil and age it, creating a new type of *aguardiente* (spirit distilled from fruits or vegetables) and named it cachaça. There are many different kinds of wood (oak, cherry and *jequitibá rosa* among them) used for ageing the spirit, each leaving different traces of taste, some with a floral flavour, others with a hint of vanilla or cinnamon.

Cachaça was considered a poor man's drink, and a disdain for it lingered for quite some time. But in Brazil there is a current wave of 'waking up' to our own cuisine and ingredients; the culture has changed, and today cachaça couldn't be more in style and caipirinhas have found a global audience.

In the USA, cachaça is also called Brazilian rum, and the distillation process is quite similar. The difference between the two is that rum is distilled from molasses (which also comes from sugar cane), while cachaça is distilled from fresh sugar cane juice. Good cachaça has an intense aroma and the flavour of fresh sugar cane.

If you would like to sniff deeper and choose from a selection of hundreds of different cachaças, step off the beach for an afternoon and visit Academia da Cachaça, a rickety bar devoted entirely to the spirit. You can taste cachaça until you end up under the table, or you can do what I do: I practise my devotion eating some *petiscos* (bar food) with a caipirinha on the side. The food at Academia da Cachaça is just as amazing as the caipirinhas.

SERVES 1

2 limes

1 tablespoon sugar

2–3 tablespoons cachaça

Ice cubes

Cut the two ends off the lime and cut the lime into medium wedges.

Using a muddler, mash the lime with the sugar, making sure you squeeze out all the juice and dissolve the sugar in the juice.

Transfer the lime mixture to a shaker. Add the cachaça and ice cubes, shake well (8 to 10 times) and pour into a large (but not tall), sturdy glass.

Serve immediately.

Suco de Mamâo com Laranja

PAPAYA AND ORANGE SMOOTHIE

Papaya is tropical, bright and buttery with a complex sweetness. The fruit pairs particularly nicely with the tang of orange. As a child, this smoothie was the first one I liked at BB Lanches, a juice store in Leblon. It is a classic juice bar offering, and I make it all the time for breakfast in my own kitchen, especially when I can find papayas from Brazil. Papayas are so sweet that this smoothie doesn't call for any added sugar, but if you like yours a little sweeter, feel free to add a dash of sugar or other sweetener.

SERVES 1

1 small papaya, deseeded and peeled

250ml fresh orange juice (from about 2 oranges)

Combine the papaya and orange juice in a blender and blend for about 2 minutes until completely smooth.

Pour into a tall highball glass and serve immediately.

RESTAURANT: BB Lanches
R. Aristides Espínola, 64 - Leblon

Rissoles de Camarão Com Catupiry

PRAWN AND CATUPIRY CHEESE TURNOVERS

RESTAURANT: Bar e Restaurante Jobi, Av. Ataulfo de Paiva, 1166 - Leblon

Located at a perfect corner of Leblon, and just steps from my family home in Rio, Jobi represents the quintessential carioca spirit. For more than 50 years, this botequim has been enchanting the city with its impeccable Portuguese cuisine, prepared in a tiny kitchen that serves extraordinary food. An order of their rissoles comes in a small tray with six turnovers and is one of the things I miss most about my life in Rio. When I go back to visit, my mother always suggests that we go to Jobi on the pretext that it is conveniently located close to our house, but in reality she is totally addicted to these rissoles. And I am too!

MAKES ABOUT 35

DOUGH

500ml full-fat milk

45g unsalted butter

1½ teaspoons salt

315g plain flour, sifted, plus extra for dusting

FILLING

2 tablespoons olive oil

225g large prawns, peeled and deveined

Sea salt and freshly ground black pepper

30g unsalted butter

1 shallot, very finely chopped

1 garlic clove, very finely chopped

1 tablespoon plain flour

175ml full-fat milk

Sea salt and freshly ground pepper

Freshly grated nutmeg

135g Catupiry cheese or cream cheese, at room temperature

500ml vegetable oil, for frying

2 medium eggs, lightly beaten

255g dried breadcrumbs

Prepare the dough. Combine the milk, butter and salt in a medium saucepan and bring to the boil. Add the flour all at once and cook, mixing with a wooden spoon, for about 3 minutes until it comes away from sides of the pan. Transfer the dough to a lightly floured surface and leave to rest for about 10 minutes until cool enough to handle. Gather the dough into a ball and knead lightly by hand until it is smooth. Divide the ball in half and flatten each half into a disc. Leave to cool completely, then wrap each disc lightly with clingfilm. Do not chill.

Prepare the filling. Heat the olive oil in a medium frying pan over a medium heat. Season the prawns with salt and pepper, add them to the pan and cook for about 1 minute each side until they just start to turn pink. Transfer to a chopping board and leave to cool for a few minutes, then roughly chop them (each prawn should be cut into 4 or 5 pieces). Place in a bowl and cover lightly with foil.

In the same pan, melt the butter over a low heat, add the shallots and cook for about 2 minutes until softened and translucent. Add the garlic and cook for about another minute until softened. Add the flour and stir with a wooden spoon, making sure everything blends together without browning. Add the milk and stir constantly for about 3 minutes until the mixture thickens. Season with salt, pepper and nutmeg. Pour into the bowl with the prawns and fold everything together. Taste, adjust the seasoning and leave to cool completely.

Have a small bowl of water and a pastry brush on hand. Place one disc of dough on a lightly floured surface and dust with flour. Roll into a 3mm-thick oval. Using a 9cm round biscuit cutter, cut out as many rounds as you can get. (You can gather the scraps and knead again, but note that this dough can easily be over-kneaded, so go gently and take care to prevent cracks from appearing.)

Place 1 tablespoon of the prawn filling onto each dough round and spread 1 teaspoon of the cheese on top. Brush a little water around the edges and fold each round in half, pressing the edges with your fingers to seal tightly. Repeat with the rest of the dough and filling. (At this point you can refrigerate the rissoles in a plastic container for up to 2 days.)

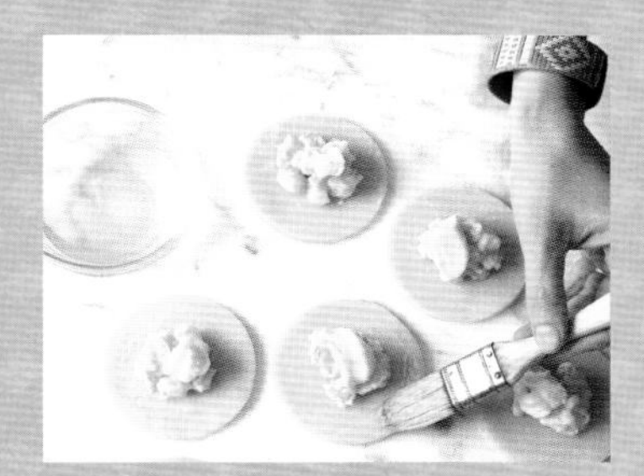

Pour the vegetable oil into a heavy-based saucepan and heat to 180°C as measured by a deep-fat thermometer.

Prepare 3 different shallow bowls: one for the eggs, one for the breadcrumbs and one for the assembled rissoles. Dip each rissole into the egg and transfer to the breadcrumbs, coating well. (I like to keep one hand wet for the eggs and the other hand dry for the breadcrumbs.)

Fry the rissoles in batches, adding as many as will fit without touching, and turning them with a long slotted spoon so that they brown evenly on all sides. Transfer to a plate lined with kitchen paper. Continue working in batches until all the rissoles are fried. Serve immediately. (You can keep the rissoles in a plastic container in the fridge for up to 3 days and reheat in a 150°C/Gas Mark 2 oven for 5–10 minutes.)

Bolinho de Bacalhau

GOLDEN SALT COD FRITTERS

These addictive fried treats are one of Rio's greatest gustatory experiences, and you can find them in just about every botequim in the city in many variations. But they have a very special meaning for Chico & Alaíde. After working at Bracarense (another fantastic botequim worth visiting) for 15 years – he as a waiter, she as a cook – Chico and Alaíde gathered their savings, rolled up their sleeves and opened this excellent botequim, doing exactly what they do best: serving and cooking bar food. It is the first of many restaurants that line Rua Dias Ferreira, one of the most buzzed-about streets in Rio. The ambience is slightly more polished than an old timer, reflecting the young age of this botequim. Creativity runs wild through Alaíde's veins, but I still love the traditional *bolinho de bacalhau*, a recipe that is just as much a part of their journey as it is part of Rio's history.

MAKES ABOUT 15

1kg salt cod

750ml cold milk

5 large (about 1.5kg) King Edward potatoes

Sea salt

1 tablespoon olive oil

2 garlic cloves, very finely chopped

1 shallot, very finely chopped

6 medium egg yolks

2 tablespoons chopped fresh parsley

Cayenne pepper

Freshly ground black pepper

Freshly grated nutmeg

500ml vegetable or rapeseed oil, for frying

RESTAURANT: Chico e Alaíde, Rua Dias Ferreira, 679 - Leblon chicoealaide.com.br

Rinse the salt cod in cold water and place it in a large container. (The volume of water should be 10–15 times the size of the cod, so use a very big container; you can cut the fish to fit the container if necessary.) Cover with cold water, cover with a tight-fitting lid and soak in the fridge for 12–24 hours, changing the water at least 3 times. Drain.

Transfer the cod to a medium saucepan and cover with the milk. Bring to the boil over a medium heat, then reduce the heat to low and cook for about 20 minutes until the cod until becomes opaque. Turn off the heat and leave to cool.

When cool enough to handle, use a slotted spoon to remove the cod and discard the milk. Flake the cod with your hands into big chunks, then shred it by either chopping with a chef's knife or pulsing in a food processor. The fish will have lost about half its weight at this point: expect about 740g shredded fish. You can now place the cod in a storage container, cover with a tight-fitting lid and refrigerate for up to 6 hours until ready to use.

Peel the potatoes and chop them. Place in a heavy-based saucepan and add cold water to cover and a pinch of salt. Cover the pan and bring to the boil, then reduce the heat to medium and simmer for 8–10 minutes until the potatoes are fork-tender. Drain, and while still hot, pass the potatoes through a ricer or food mill – you will have 1.25kg mashed potatoes. Assemble the cod fritters while the potatoes are still warm.

Combine the shredded cod and mashed potatoes in a large bowl. Add the olive oil, garlic, shallot, egg yolks and parsley. If the batter gets too difficult to mix by hand, you can use an electric mixer fitted with the paddle attachment at low speed. Season with cayenne, salt, pepper and nutmeg.

Roll the mixture into 2.5cm balls, place them on baking sheets and refrigerate for 30 minutes while you prepare the oil for frying.

COOKING TIP: This may seem like a lot of fritters, but one piece of salt cod yields a lot of these bite-sized treats. This is a perfect party hors d'oeuvre; or make them all and freeze half in an airtight container for up to 3 months; thaw and reheat in a 150°C/Gas Mark 2 oven for 5–10 minutes.

Meanwhile, preheat the oven to 110°C/Gas Mark ¼.

Pour the oil into a heavy-based saucepan and heat it to 180°C, as measured by a deep-fat thermometer. Drop in 12–14 cod balls – only as many as will fit without touching each other. Fry, turning occasionally with a long slotted spoon and making sure both sides are browned evenly, for about 5 minutes. Transfer to a baking sheet lined with kitchen paper. Continue working in batches until all the fritters are fried; keep the finished batches in the oven as you go. When all the fritters are fried, serve immediately.

INGREDIENT NOTE: When buying salt cod, look for a piece that's very meaty and trim off the dark parts around the belly and tail before soaking.

Salada de Bacalhau, Feijão Branco, e Cebola Roxa

SALT COD AND WHITE BEAN SALAD WITH RED ONIONS

Tapas in Spain, *petiscos* in Brazil: the two have a lot in common. Venga is one of the few botequims that has embraced the spirit of Rio with a Spanish influence. Before it opened its doors in 2009, Fernando Kaplan, one of the partners, travelled to Spain to research the world of tapas, and the result is simply terrific: Spain on a plate as seen from Rio de Janeiro. The restaurant is charming, thanks to a world of bottles decorating the walls, and a set-up of bar tables, standard dining tables and communal tables add to the atmosphere; conversations sparkle and flow while you wait for the food to arrive. This recipe is inspired by a delicious salad I ate there, a perfect meeting of carioca and Spanish cuisines.

SERVES 6–8

450g dried cannellini beans, picked and rinsed

1 large red onion, halved and thinly sliced

1 tablespoon sherry vinegar

½ teaspoon salt

2 tablespoons olive oil

1kg salt cod, soaked, drained and cooked (see page 20 for instructions)

10g fresh parsley, chopped

Dressing

Juice of ½ lime

2 tablespoons sherry vinegar

1 small garlic clove, mashed into a paste

Tabasco sauce

125ml olive oil, plus extra for drizzling

Place the beans in a large saucepan or pressure cooker. Add about 2 litres water, cover the pan or lock the pressure cooker and cook until the beans are cooked but not mushy – about 1½ hours for a saucepan, 30 minutes for a pressure cooker. Drain and discard the water. Spread the beans on a large plate to cool.

Put the onion slices in a bowl and add enough water to cover, about 250ml. Add the vinegar and salt and leave to stand for 40 minutes.

Drain the onions and discard the water. Heat the olive oil in a small frying pan over a low heat, add the onions and cook for about 6 minutes, stirring frequently, until softened. They will remain bright red – that's what you want. Transfer to a plate and leave to cool.

Roughly chop the salt cod, then shred with your fingers, discarding any fatty or dark pieces.

Make the dressing. Combine the lime juice, vinegar, garlic, and a few drops of Tabasco in a small bowl, then add the olive oil in a steady stream, whisking constantly until emulsified.

Place the beans and cod in a bowl. Add the red onions and parsley. Pour the dressing over and mix well with a rubber spatula. Taste and adjust the seasoning with salt and pepper. Cover and refrigerate for at least 2 hours to develop the flavours. Bring to room temperature 30 minutes before serving.

COOKING TIP: I prefer to cook dried white beans, but you can use canned beans to save time.

RESTAURANT: Venga, R. Dias Ferreira, 113 - Leblon
venga.com.br

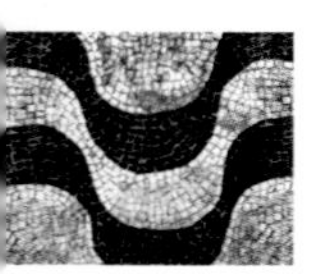

Frango à Passarinho
BRAZILIAN-STYLE FRIED CHICKEN

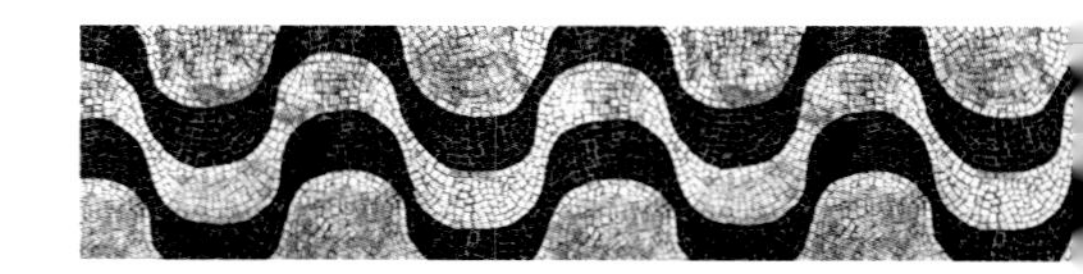

Frango à passarinho translates to 'chicken bird style', referring to the small pieces the chicken is cut into. This dish is inspired by Bracarense, an iconic botequim, and any home cook can handle this simple recipe. It's fried chicken at its most basic – golden and crunchy, garnished with sliced or chopped garlic and fresh parsley. I often make it in my American kitchen for my family when I am looking for a way to add a Brazilian twist to a chicken dish, and then my kids add their own American twist by dipping it in a side of barbecue sauce. Between one twist and another, an amazing dinner is the result, and the platter goes back to the kitchen absolutely clean.

SERVES 6–8 AS A STARTER OR 4 AS A MAIN COURSE

1 whole chicken (1.3–1.8kg)

1 teaspoon finely grated lime zest

60ml fresh lime juice

350ml bottle of beer, such as Stella Artois

500ml rapeseed or vegetable oil, for frying

Sea salt and freshly ground black pepper

150g plain flour

4–5 garlic cloves, thinly sliced or roughly chopped

3 tablespoons chopped fresh parsley

Remove the skin from the chicken and cut it into 5cm pieces. Place in a bowl and add the lime zest, lime juice and beer. Cover with clingfilm and leave to marinate for 1 hour at room temperature. Drain the chicken, discarding the liquid, and spread the chicken pieces on a baking sheet lined with kitchen paper. Air-dry for at least 5 minutes. It's okay if some of the lime zest remains on the chicken.

Heat the oil in a deep, wide frying pan over a medium heat until it registers 180°C on a deep-fat thermometer.

Season the chicken with salt and pepper on all sides. Place the flour in a large, shallow bowl and season with salt and pepper. Roll the chicken pieces in the flour, shake off some but not all of the excess flour and arrange the pieces on a baking sheet.

Working in batches, add the chicken pieces one at a time to the oil, only putting in as many as will fit in the pan without touching, and cook for about 8 minutes for each batch, turning the chicken with tongs so that it's golden on all sides.

Transfer the chicken pieces to a baking sheet lined with kitchen paper.

Quickly add the garlic to the same oil in the pan and fry, stirring constantly, for about 2 minutes until it just starts to turn golden. Remove the garlic from the oil with a slotted spoon, sprinkle the garlic over the chicken and finish with the parsley. Serve immediately.

RESTAURANT: Bar Bracarense,
Rua Jose Linhares,
85 - Leblon

Bacalhau à Gomes Sá

BAKED SALT COD WITH POTATOES, ONIONS, EGGS AND OLIVES

Dinner at Antiquarius serves rustic Portuguese cuisine at a sophisticated level, with dishes that are based on tradition and service that is deeply personalised. When visiting Antiquarius, ask to meet Manuel Pires, or Manuelzinho, one of the most beloved waiters in of all Rio. His descriptions of their cod dishes are mouthwatering, and *bacalhau à Gomes Sá* is a highlight on the menu. The name of this dish comes from a cook named José Luiz Gomes de Sá, who created this recipe in the early 1900s while working at a restaurant in the city of Porto, Portugal. The dish was brought to Brazil by Portuguese immigrants and today is one of the most well-known cod recipes in both countries.

SERVES 8–10

900g salt cod, soaked, drained and cooked (see page 20 for instructions)

590ml cold milk

900g small young or Charlotte potatoes, halved and sliced 2cm thick

Sea salt

300ml extra virgin olive oil, plus 3 tablespoons

3 onions, thinly sliced

10g fresh parsley, chopped

Freshly ground black pepper

3 hard-boiled eggs, shelled and thinly sliced

45g kalamata olives, pitted and halved

RESTAURANT: Antiquarius, R. Aristides Espínola, 19 - Leblon

Preheat the oven to 180°C. Lightly coat a 23cm x 33cm baking dish with cooking spray.

Place the salt cod in a medium saucepan, cutting the fish to fit the pan if necessary. Cover the salt cod with the milk. Bring to the boil over a high heat, then reduce the heat to low and cook, covered, for about 15 minutes until the fish becomes opaque. Turn the heat off and leave the fish to rest in the milk, covered, for at least 20 minutes. Using a slotted spoon, remove the fish and discard the milk. Flake the fish with your hands into small chunks or pulse it in a food processor for just a few seconds. Place the fish in a storage container, cover with a tight-fitting lid and refrigerate for up to 6 hours until ready to use.

Place the potatoes in a large, heavy-based saucepan. Cover with cold water by at least 2.5cm and add a large pinch of salt. Bring to the boil over a high heat, then reduce the heat to medium and simmer for 12–15 minutes until fork-tender. Drain, then spread the potatoes over a plate. Set aside.

Heat the 3 tablespoons of olive oil in a large frying pan over a low heat. Add the onions and cook, stirring occasionally, for 15–20 minutes until softened and translucent. Resist the temptation to use a high heat to avoid browning them. If they do begin to brown, add a tablespoon of water. In a large bowl, combine the shredded salt cod, onions and potatoes. Mix in 60ml of the remaining olive oil and the parsley. Taste, and season lightly with salt (the cod will already be salty) and pepper.

Spread the mixture evenly across the prepared baking dish. Drizzle the remaining 240ml olive oil over the top. Place in the oven and bake for 15–20 minutes until bubbling hot. Remove the dish from the oven, distribute the eggs and olives all over and return the dish to the oven for a further 10 minutes to heat through. Serve hot.

INGREDIENT NOTE: When buying salt cod, look for a piece that looks very meaty and trim away the dark parts around the belly and tail before soaking the fish.

Dadinhos de Tapioca com Queijo

CRISPY TAPIOCA CHEESE FRITTERS

Zuka is a very versatile restaurant: whatever purpose – business lunch, romantic date, dinner with friends – it fits the occasion. The menu sprinkles exotic Brazilian ingredients with dishes that are internationally familiar. I was interviewing Chef Ludmilla Soeiro for my blog when I first tried these crunchy tapioca fritters. I couldn't get over how remarkably delicious they were and couldn't wait to try the recipe at home. I made them with Parmesan, cured and grated Minas cheese, Brazilian coalho cheese and Greek halloumi. My favourite is Parmesan, but they all produce a great fritter. Ludmilla told me that she learned this recipe from Chef Rodrigo Oliveira, based in São Paulo – (see page 127 for another of his recipes) – proving that good recipes travel fast.

MAKES ABOUT 45

- 135g Parmesan cheese, finely grated
- 125g small tapioca pearls
- 250ml full-fat milk
- Sea salt and freshly ground black pepper
- Freshly grated nutmeg
- Pinch of paprika
- 500ml vegetable oil, for frying

Line a small (1-litre) baking dish with clingfilm, leaving an overhang on all sides. Be sure it's deep enough to hold the batter.

Combine the cheese and tapioca in a medium bowl. Bring the milk to the boil in a small saucepan. Pour the hot milk over the tapioca and mix with a rubber spatula; the tapioca will immediately start to release starch and the dough will become thick and pasty. Season with salt, pepper and nutmeg and the paprika. Pour into the prepared baking dish and spread evenly. Immediately cover with clingfilm to prevent a skin from forming. Leave to cool at room temperature for at least 1 hour, then refrigerate for at least 2 hours or up to 5 days.

Pour the vegetable oil into a heavy-based saucepan and heat to 180°C, as measured by a deep-fat thermometer.

Unmould the tapioca dough onto a chopping board. Using a long knife, trim the edges and cut the dough into neat 2.5cm cubes.

Fry the tapioca cubes in batches, adding only as many as will fit without touching and turning occasionally with a long slotted spoon to prevent them from sticking together, for about 3 minutes until evenly browned on all sides. Transfer to a baking sheet lined with kitchen paper. Continue working in batches until all the fritters are fried. Serve the fritters immediately.

RESTAURANT: Zuka,
R. Dias Ferreira,
233 - Leblon zuka.com.br

COOKING TIP: You can bake these in a 180°C/ Gas Mark 4 oven for 12–15 minutes, but frying brings the best crispness to the plate. Serve them with red pepper jam if you like.

INGREDIENT NOTE: If you can get your hands on the Brazilian tapioca flour from Yoki or Bascom's, use it instead of the tapioca pearls and these will taste ultra-extraordinaire.

Brigadeiro

SWEET MILK AND CHOCOLATE FUDGE

This iconic Brazilian sweet was named after Eduardo Gomes, a brigadier who, in the early 1900s, was admired for his good looks and notoriously loved chocolate. When sweetened condensed milk was invented (in Switzerland) and brought to Brazil, chefs created this fudge using the sweet milk and chocolate. This recipe is inspired by the *brigadeiro* sold at Colher de Pau. Eating their sweets is a journey into the past, and Colher de Pau is a landmark in Rio. Thirty-something years have passed, and the brigadeiro of my childhood is still there, as fudgy, handsome and seducing as ever.

MAKES ABOUT 20

397g can sweetened condensed milk

15g unsalted butter

40g cocoa powder (preferably Giardelli)

80g chocolate vermicelli

RESTAURANT: Colher de Pau
R. Rita Ludolf, 90 - Leblon
colherdepaurio.com.br

Combine the condensed milk, butter and cocoa in a medium, heavy-based saucepan. Bring to the boil over a medium heat. Reduce the heat to low and cook, stirring constantly with a wooden spoon, for 8–10 minutes until the mixture is thick and creamy. You'll know it's ready when you swirl the pan around and the whole mixture slides as one soft piece and leaves a thick residue on the base of the pan.

Slide the mixture into a bowl. Don't scrape the pan – you don't want to include any of the burnt batter on the base of the pan. Leave to cool to room temperature, then cover and refrigerate for at least 4 hours, or preferably overnight.

Scoop the mixture by the teaspoonful and, using your hands, roll it into little balls about 2cm in diameter.

Place the vermicelli in a shallow dish. Pass the brigadeiros, 4–6 at a time, through the vermicelli, making sure they stick and cover the entire surface. Eat immediately or store in an airtight container for up to 3 days, after which the condensed milk will crystallise (making a crunchier brigadeiro that is still okay to eat).

Toalha Felpuda

COCONUT LAYER CAKE WITH COCONUT PASTRY CREAM AND MERINGUE FROSTING

This coconut cake is based on the one you'll find at Colher de Pau (see box on page 27), a sweet little store in Leblon. The translation of *toalha felpuda* is 'furry towel', referring to the white blanket of coconut frosting that covers the cake. From the very first bite, you'll recognise that this is a coconut cake unlike any other. There is something about it that allows you to eat without feeling the weight of food entering your body, as if you were eating coconut clouds. That's because there is no flour – only potato starch – and no butter in the frosting. Both the pastry cream and the cake benefit from chilling time before assembling; the pastry cream could even be made the day before and refrigerated overnight.

SERVES 8–10

plain flour, for dusting

6 medium eggs, separated, at room temperature

2 medium egg yolks, at room temperature

340g sugar

salt

330g potato starch, sifted

COCONUT PASTRY CREAM

3 medium egg yolks

5 tablespoons sugar

2 tablespoons cornflour

400ml coconut milk

30g unsalted butter, at room temperature, plus extra for greasing

150ml double cream

50g grated fresh coconut or unsweetened desiccated coconut

COCONUT MERINGUE

6 medium egg whites

300g caster sugar

1 teaspoon vanilla extract

360ml coconut milk, brought just to the boil, then cooled

100g grated fresh coconut

Set an oven shelf in the middle position and preheat the oven to 180°C/Gas Mark 4. Butter a 25cm round cake tin 5cm deep, line the base with baking parchment, butter the lining paper and dust with flour, shaking off excess.

Make the cake. Beat all 8 egg yolks with 100g of the sugar in the bowl of an electric mixer fitted with the whisk attachment until the mixture thickens and turns pale yellow.

In a separate bowl, beat the 6 egg whites with a pinch of salt on medium speed until frothy. With the mixer running, gradually sprinkle the remaining 240g sugar and beat until soft peaks forms.

Using a rubber spatula, fold one-third of the egg whites into the egg yolk mixture, then fold in the remaining egg whites. Slowly sprinkle the potato starch over the mixture and fold carefully with a rubber spatula, scraping all the way to the base of the bowl on every pass to prevent the potato starch from accumulating or forming lumps.

Scrape the batter into the prepared cake tin and smooth the top with an angled palette knife. Bake, rotating the pan halfway through, for 40–45 minutes until a skewer inserted into the centre comes out clean.

Leave to cool in the pan on a wire rack for 30 minutes, then turn the cake out and leave it to cool completely on the rack. Cover the cake loosely with clingfilm and refrigerate for at least 5 hours.

Make the coconut pastry cream. Whisk together the egg yolks, 3 tablespoons of the sugar and the cornflour in a medium bowl.

Bring the coconut milk to a simmer over a medium heat in a medium saucepan. Whisking constantly, pour the hot coconut milk into the egg yolk mixture, gradually at first to temper it, and then more quickly. Transfer the mixture back to the saucepan and cook over a low heat, whisking constantly, for about 4 minutes until it reaches a pudding-like consistency. Transfer to a bowl and leave to stand for 10 minutes, stirring occasionally. Whisk in the butter.

Whip the cream with the remaining 2 tablespoons sugar until fluffy in the bowl of the electric mixer fitted with the whisk attachment. Fold the whipped cream into the coconut pastry cream, then fold in the grated

INGREDIENT NOTES:
The coconut used in the pastry cream can be dried, but try to use freshly grated coconut to cover the cake. It makes a big difference!

Different brands of potato starch vary in weight, so measure the quantity accurately. I use Ener-G potato starch.

coconut. Press a piece of clingfilm directly over the cream to prevent a crust from forming and refrigerate until firm, for at least 2 hours or preferably overnight.

Make the coconut meringue. Combine the egg whites and sugar in the bowl of an electric mixer and set it over a saucepan of simmering water (the bowl should not touch the water). Whisk constantly until the mixture is warm to the touch and slightly foamy and the sugar is completely dissolved. Remove the bowl from the pan and set it on the base of the mixer fitted with the whisk attachment. Whisk on medium-high speed for about 10 minutes until the mixture is fluffy, glossy and completely cooled. Whisk in the vanilla.

To assemble the cake, use a long serrated knife to trim the top and sides of the cake, then cut the cake into 3 equal horizontal layers. Set one layer cut side up on a card disc and brush generously with the coconut milk. Spread half of the coconut pastry cream over the cake with an angled palette knife. Top with another cake layer, brush with coconut milk and spread the remaining coconut pastry cream on top. Set the third cake layer on top cut side down and frost the sides and top of the cake with the coconut meringue. Gently pat the grated coconut all over the cake.

2

IPANEMA

A TRIBUTE TO THE FARMERS' MARKET

When I am in Rio, I spend a lot of time browsing the city's many food markets. Not just the street markets that are found each day in a different Zona Sul neighbourhood, but also the fish market in Niterói, the Feira de São Cristovão and Cadeg in Benfica.

To me these markets are some of the most enlightening, energising and generous places in the world.

When I was a kid, I would join my mother at the gym in Ipanema, and we would always make a stop at the same farmers' market on Fridays. I remember that 'aha!' moment when I realised that the orange roulade, a treat I was crazy for, was actually prepared by the Portuguese lady behind the stand. I am still crazy for it, and you can try my version in this chapter. As a young teenager attracted by anything edible, I took over the role of going to the market for my mother, whose favourite part of the market was the flower stand; we never had an official agreement, but as my mother saw my growing enthusiasm for food, she eventually passed the baton to me.

But it wasn't until my late teenage years, when I started cooking more seriously, that I really became a market aficionada. Where else could I learn about salt cod or bond with a lady over a shared love of orange roulade? When I want to learn about new ingredients, the first thing I do is go to the market to figure out what am I going to prepare and how to cook it.

I also enjoy the characters and personalities. The shouting, the tastings,

the way a produce vendor cuts a mango or a melon to entice you to buy his or her fruits and vegetables. Each vendor represents a different face of Brazil: the *cupuaçú*, which comes from the Amazon, is sold by a native Amazonian; the salt cod by a Portuguese; and the *dendê* (palm) oil by an African-Brazilian. Between the laughter of the vendors and the chaos of the cariocas rushing about for the freshest ingredients, you leave the market with a sense that Rio is the most magical of cities.

Over the years I have learned that there is no tradition of sharing recipes in Brazil. The recipes are handed down by generation, and people are not about to give their secret recipes away – especially to someone who makes a living from recipe writing. As much as I disagree with this practice, it has forced me to be a better cook as I try to replicate the baked goods I've tasted at the market at home.

Rio's markets are places of hard work and early rising. I have seen men carrying impossibly huge buckets of ice to prepare a nice display of fish, and I have seen women peel and chop piles of vegetables to bag them perfectly. Grating coconut may last all morning long, because no one wants to do this job at home, but much coconut is needed to prepare the coconut-based dishes you'll find at the market. It all starts at the crack of dawn, so that by 7am everything looks gorgeous.

Rio's markets are also places of beauty. Food and people connect intensely. I see housewives buying produce for the family dinner, and I see beautiful cut-up guavas perfuming the air. I notice the curves of a pumpkin, and it reminds of a woman rolling a wagon full of groceries. I see women coming to the market straight from the gym. I see the wrinkles of a chayote, and those in the eyes of a fisherman. I see colours I didn't know existed, fruit I have never tasted and people who are as passionate about cooking as I am.

I've learned a lot about life in Rio's markets. Vendors need to sell their items, customers need to buy food and there is a world of choices at our feet. The markets have taught me how to negotiate for a better price, how to choose the best produce and how to wait for the next stand. But most of all, markets have taught me about human relationships.

GREAT MARKETS IN RIO

Farmers' Markets:

Mondays:	Rua Henrique Dumont, Ipanema
Tuesdays:	Praça General Osório, Leblon
Wednesdays:	Rua General San Martin, Leblon
Thursdays:	Aterro do Flamengo, Botafogo
Fridays:	Praça Nossa Senhora da Paz, Ipanema

Feira de São Cristóvão

I vividly remember my first visit to the market in São Cristóvão. I entered by the Luiz Gonzaga statue at the market's entrance, to be drawn into a riot of vivid colours and foods from different regions of Brazil – food that might seem exotic to just about any carioca. Among the many market treasures, I found a stand with more than ten different types of yucca flour.

feiradesaocristovao.org.br

Mercado de Peixes São Pedro in Niterói

Located on the other side of the bridge across from Rio, this fish market is recognised as the most important in the state of Rio de Janeiro. It supplies most restaurants and supermarkets in the region, but it also sells directly to the customer. The building holds more than 20 different stands and several restaurants specialising in fish are located on the second floor. You can buy fish downstairs, bring it to the restaurant and they will prepare it fresh for you. Most of the fish in the market is sold by 2pm.

Mercado de Peixes São Pedro, Rua Visconde do Rio Branco, 55, Niterói, Rio de Janeiro
Hours of Operation:
Tuesdays to Saturdays, 6am–6pm
Sundays, 6am–12pm

Feira Hippie Ipanema

Although this market is mostly about décor, arts and crafts, there are a few food stands on the corner of Prudente de Morais Street. My favourite are the *baianas* selling **acarajés** (bean fritters).

FeiraHippieIpanema.com

Limonada Suíssa

BRAZILIAN-STYLE LIMEADE

Lemonade is a drink adored in all parts of the world. In the United States lemonade is the quintessential flavour of summer, and if you like it, you will love this Brazilian version made with limes. Aside from its beautiful pastel green colour, what I love about this classic Brazilian refreshment is that it makes use of the whole lime, both the juice and peel with all its aromatic oils. I love to order a limonada at Polis Sucos after a visit to the gym.

MAKES 1 TALL GLASS

2 limes

50g sugar

360ml water

Ice cubes

RESTAURANT: Polis Sucos
R. Maria Quitéria,
70 - Rio de Janeiro

Remove both the ends of the limes and cut each lime into eighths. Place in a blender, add the sugar and water and blend for 3–4 minutes until very smooth. Set a fine-mesh sieve over a tall glass and pour in the limeade, pressing the solids against the sieve to extract all the liquid. Discard the solids. Add 2 or 3 ice cubes and serve immediately.

INGREDIENT NOTE: The name of this recipe translates to ;Swiss limeade'; this is because the original recipe called for sweetened condensed milk, imported from Switzerland. Today it is prepared with sugar instead.

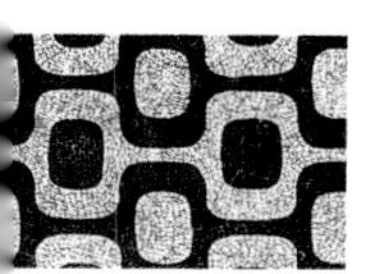

Biscoito O Globo
YUCCA COOKIE

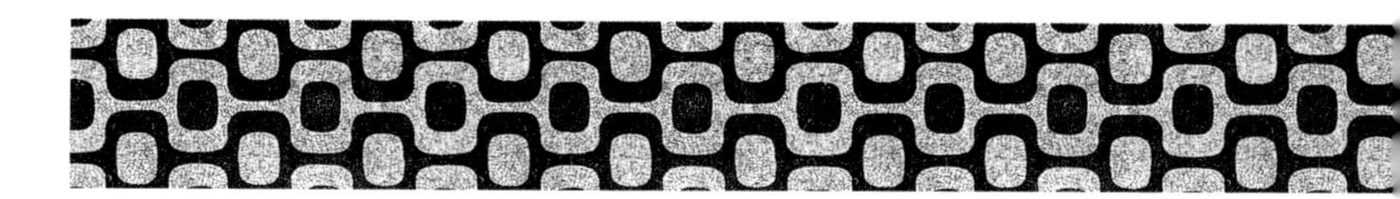

The story of *biscoito globo* begins in 1953, when the three brothers Ponce (Milton, Jaime and João) went to live with a cousin who was a baker in São Paulo. Their cousin taught them to make this delicious cookie, which they soon brought to Rio. The cookie went from the aisles of bakeries to the sand of Rio's beaches and there isn't a single carioca who doesn't love *biscoito globo*. This recipe is inspired by this bland but very addictive cookie. You can make it with vegetable oil or with olive oil. Originally the cookie is plump, fluffy and round – almost the size of an American bagel – but you can also pipe them into sticks, which is easier to do at home as it prevents the cookies from expanding into one big mass.

MAKES ABOUT 60

405g sour manioc starch (*povilho azedo*)

1 tablespoon sea salt

70ml vegetable oil

125ml full-fat milk

1 medium egg

Preheat the oven to 180°C/Gas Mark 4. Line 2 baking sheets with baking paper or a silicone mat.

Place the manioc starch in the bowl of an electric mixer fitted with the paddle attachment. Add the salt and 125ml of water and break the starch up with your fingers. In a small saucepan, bring another 125ml of water and the oil to the boil. Immediately pour the hot liquid over the manioc starch and turn the machine on low speed. Beat until the mixture looks like a coarse meal, about 1 minute.

Slowly pour in the milk. Add the egg and beat until the dough turns pale and creamy, 3 to 4 minutes.

Stop the machine and scrape the dough into a piping bag fitted with a plain round no. 6 piping tube. Pipe the batter into rounds, leaving about 1.25cm between each cookie.

Bake for 25 to 35 minutes, until the cookies rise and are slightly golden. Turn off the heat and leave them in the oven with the door ajar for 30 minutes.

Remove them from the oven and cool completely before serving.

Pão de Queijo

PARMESAN CHEESE ROLLS

RESTAURANT: Esplanada Grill, R. Barão da Torre, 600 - Ipanema esplanadagrill.com.br

I'll never forget the first time I ate ostrich. It was at Esplanada Grill, located in the gleaming corner of Rua Barão da Torre and Anibal de Mendonca. The meat was gamey, soft and juicy, sealing my taste for wild meats that day. Esplanada Grill doesn't look like your typical *churrascaria* – because it's not. Esplanada Grill built its reputation out of a fine à la carte menu serving exquisite Brazilian beef as well as exotic meats such as *javali* (wild boar), *pirarucu* (a fish from the Amazon River) and the above-mentioned ostrich. But one of my favourite treats at Esplanada is the *pão de queijo*. It is so cheesy that I sometimes find it impossible to save room to appreciate some of the best meat in Rio.

Much has been made of Brazilians' fascination with *pão de queijo*. From Belém do Pará in the north of the country to Rio Grande do Sul in the south, and anywhere in between, *pão de queijo* has the power to ignite conversations and direct dinner choices. This dish is the result of yucca alchemy – a golf ball-sized little roll that is chewy, cheesy and steamy, almost succulent – and it's quite difficult to eat just one.

Makes 35

630g sour manioc starch (*polvilho azedo*)

250ml water

250ml full-fat milk

180ml vegetable or rapeseed oil

2 teaspoons salt

3 medium eggs

185g Parmesan cheese, finely grated

Freshly grated nutmeg

⅛ teaspoon cayenne pepper

Freshly ground black pepper

INGREDIENT NOTE: The main ingredient in *pão de queijo* is *polvilho azedo*, or sour manioc starch, see the Glossary on page 196. I use Yoki brand, which is easily available online.

Place the manioc starch in the bowl of an electric mixer fitted with the paddle attachment. Set aside.

Combine the water, milk, oil and salt in a small saucepan and bring to the boil. Immediately pour the hot liquid mixture into the manioc starch all at once and turn the machine to low speed. Mix for about 2 minutes until the dough is smooth and the starch is incorporated. Pause the machine and add the eggs. Continue to mix at low speed for about 5 minutes until the dough develops structure and turns pale yellow. The dough will be sticky.

Add the cheese and mix until well incorporated. Season with nutmeg, the cayenne and a few twists of pepper. Transfer the dough to a bowl, cover with clingfilm and refrigerate for at least 2 hours.

Preheat the oven to 180°C/Gas Mark 4. Line 2 baking sheets with baking parchment.

Wet your hands with olive oil or flour your hands with manioc starch. Use an ice cream scoop to make 2.5cm balls and roll the balls into shape with your hands. Place the balls on the prepared baking sheets, leaving 4–5cm between each. (At this point you can store them in a zip-seal freezer bag and freeze them for up to 3 months.)

Place the cheese rolls in the oven and bake, rotating the sheets halfway through the baking time, for 12–14 minutes until they puff up and are lightly golden brown.

Remove the rolls from the oven and place them in a basket lined with a clean tea towel. Serve immediately while they are still at their warmest and chewiest.

Pasteis de Carne

DEEP-FRIED BEEF EMPANADAS

Pasteis (emapanadas) are great any time of day, but in my experience some of the best ones are sold at the farmers' market in Ipanema for lunch, accompanied by a fresh cup of sugar cane juice. These *pasteis* are rectangular in shape and a lot larger than the versions generally made at home or in restaurants, and that is the version I am presenting here. While you can prepare your own pastry dough and roll it into thin discs, I suggest using shop-bought pastry discs – as is done in every household in Rio – or egg roll or wonton wrappers, as it is a lot of work to get the dough as thin as you'll need it for this recipe.

MAKES ABOUT 15

3 tablespoons olive oil

1 small onion, finely chopped

3 spring onions, white and green parts, finely chopped

3 garlic cloves, very finely chopped

1 teaspoon dried oregano

Sea salt and freshly ground black pepper

340g steak mince

400g can whole tomatoes, deseeded and chopped (reserve about 125ml juice)

2 tablespoons chopped fresh parsley

1 packet store-bought *massa de pastel* (ready-made pastel dough; see Note) or egg roll or wonton wrappers

700ml vegetable or rapeseed oil, for frying

Heat the olive oil in a large frying pan over a medium heat. Add the onion and spring onions and cook for about 2 mintues until softened and translucent. Stir in the garlic, add the oregano and season lightly with salt and pepper.

Add the mince and cook, breaking it up with a wooden spoon, for about 5 minutes until no longer pink. Add the tomatoes and the reserved juice. Reduce the heat to low and cook, stirring occasionally, for about 10 minutes until the liquid is reduced but the mixture is still moist. Mix in the fresh parsley. Spread onto a plate to cool completely.

Lay out about 5 pieces of dough at a time on a work surface, keeping the thin film attached to each layer. Place about 1½ tablespoons of the meat filling onto each piece of dough. Moisten the edges of the disc with water and fold over to form a half-moon shape. Crimp tightly with a fork to secure the edges. At this point the film will still be around each pastel, keeping it moist. Repeat until the filling and pastry discs are used.

Pour the oil for frying into a very large, heavy-based pan and heat to 180°C, as measured by a deep-fat thermometer. Carefully remove the clingfilm from each pastel when you are ready to fry. Drop 2 or 3 of the *pasteis* in at a time, and use a slotted spoon to baste oil around them constantly so that you are frying both sides at the same time. Keep basting and turning for about 2 minutes until they are light golden brown (they will get a little darker as they cool). Transfer to a baking sheet lined with kitchen paper while you prepare the remainder. Serve immediately.

INGREDIENT NOTE: *Massa de pastel pronta* (ready-made pastel dough) is packed with either square or round wrappers layered in clingfilm; you can use either one here. You can find it in Brazilian stores or online, or you can substitute wonton wrappers and the result will be just as good.

Feijoada
BRAZILIAN BLACK BEAN STEW

There are various theories as to the origin of *feijoada*. Some believe it was created by African-Brazilians during colonial times using leftovers from animal parts; others believe the dish was inspired by European meat and bean stews; and still others say that *feijoada* first became popular in the *favelas* (shanty towns) of Rio. Today the origin of *feijoada* means little to most modern cariocas, but has become a habit on some Saturdays and a desperate craving on others.

Saturdays in Rio were made for *feijoada*. Every Saturday, the Hotel Caesar Park serves a stunning version, with various meats presented in many cauldrons, the clay pots that are just as characteristic of the dish as the dish itself, and which lend an earthy taste to the food.

A feijoada includes everything your mother ever told you to trim from a piece of meat and move to the side of your plate. This is a dish of bold temptation and prompt surrender for carnivores. It's hard to eat with much finesse around glistening pounds of pork shoulder, ham hocks, pig's ears and *carne seca* (dried meat). And that's one of the things I love most about this dish: you can see into people's inner personalities when they eat it.

SERVES 8–10

225g *carne seca*

450g pork shoulder, cut into 5cm pieces

450g pork belly, cut into 5cm strips

340g smoked ham hock

115g pancetta, cubed

675g linguiça, chorizo or other spicy fresh sausage

450g dried black beans, picked and rinsed

3 tablespoons olive oil

5 garlic cloves, very finely chopped

1 large onion, finely diced

2 spring onions, white and green parts, chopped

2 fresh bay leaves

Sea salt and freshly ground black pepper

Cayenne pepper

Paprika

Freshly grated nutmeg

10g fresh coriander, chopped

10g fresh parsley, chopped

If using *carne seca*, rinse it under cold running water, place it in a bowl, cover with water and refrigerate for 12–24 hours, changing the water at least 3 times. Drain the carne seca and discard the water.

Place all the meats in a large saucepan and add water to cover by 2.5cm. Place over a high heat and bring to the boil, then reduce the heat to low and simmer for 1–1½ hours. The meats will be done at different times; check frequently, and, using a slotted spoon, transfer each meat to a bowl as it's done and cover with foil to keep it moist. You are looking for the meat to be tender, but keep in mind that it will be cooking for another hour or so with the black beans.

Place the beans in a large pan or pressure cooker. Add about 6 litres water, cover the pan or lock the pressure cooker and cook until the beans are cooked through but not mushy – about 1½ hours for a pan, 30 minutes for a pressure cooker. Reserve the beans and water in the pan.

In a very large pan, heat the olive oil over a medium heat, add the garlic and cook for about 1 minute until it just starts to turn golden. Add the onion and spring onions and cook for about 5 minutes until softened and translucent. Add the bay leaves, season with salt, pepper, cayenne, paprika and nutmeg and cook for about 3 minutes until fragrant.

Pour the beans and all the liquid into the pan with the vegetables. Add the meats and any juices that have accumulated. Bring to a simmer over a low heat and simmer gently, checking frequently, making sure the liquid level is just right; not too soupy, not too dry. Continue cooking for 1–1½ hours until the flavours meld together. While the feijoada is cooking, prepare the rice, spring greens and toasted manioc flour.

Wash the rice in cold water several times, going back and forth between a bowl and a colander, until the water becomes fairly clear. Leave the rice to stand in the colander to air-dry for 5 minutes. Heat 2 tablespoons of the olive oil in a medium saucepan over a low heat, add the onion and cook for about 2 minutes until it just starts to become

recipe continues overleaf

ACCOMPANIMENTS

370g basmati or jasmine rice

5 tablespoons extra virgin olive oil

1 medium onion, finely diced

Sea salt and freshly ground black pepper

1 bunch of spring greens

3 garlic cloves, very finely chopped

30g unsalted butter

275g manioc flour (*farinha de mandioca fina*)

4 spring onions, finely chopped, green parts reserved to garnish

5 navel oranges, peeled and cut into segments, to garnish

COOKING TIP: *Feijoada* might seem like a lot of work, but this recipe is an easy one – you just add a bunch of meats to a pot, cover with water, and cook for 1 to 1 ½ hours. At the same time, you have a separate pot of beans cooking, preferably in a pressure cooker. You then combine them to simmer for another 1 to 1½ hours while the meats and beans share flavours. Seasoning the meats a day ahead will give an even greater depth of flavour.

fragrant. Add the rice and stir with a wooden spoon until the grains are covered in fat and shiny. Add 700ml water and 2 teaspoons salt and partially cover the pan. Bring to the boil over a high heat, then reduce the heat to low and cook for about 15 minutes until the rice is tender.

Trim the stems and thick centre ribs from the spring greens and discard them. Stack a few leaves and roll them tightly into a cigar shape. Cut into very thin strips crossways and place the strips in a bowl. Repeat with the remaining leaves. Fill a bowl with ice and water, then fill a large saucepan with water and bring it to the boil. Add about 1 tablespoon salt, then add the greens and blanch for 30–60 seconds until wilted. Drain, transfer to the ice bath to cool, then drain again.

In a medium saucepan, heat 1 tablespoon of the olive oil over a medium heat. Add the garlic and cook for about 2 minutes until it just starts to turn golden. Add the greens (you might need to do this in batches) and stir to coat them in the oil. Season with salt and pepper, add about 60ml water and cook for about 3 minutes until the greens are soft but still bright green.

Melt the butter in a medium saucepan over a low heat. Add the manioc flour and toast, stirring constantly, for 8–10 minutes until it is a light golden colour. Watch carefully, as the flour can burn easily. Remove from the heat and set aside.

Heat the remaining 2 tablespoons olive oil in a large non-stick frying pan over a medium heat. Add the spring onions and cook for about 3 minutes until they just start to soften, Stir in the toasted manioc flour. Season with salt and pepper, pour into a serving dish and garnish with the reserved spring onions.

Place a mound of rice on a plate and ladle the beans with meats on top. Add the toasted manioc flour and spring greens alongside, and garnish with the fresh coriander and parsley and navel orange segments.

INGREDIENT NOTE: *Feijoada* is a blank canvas for meat choices – I have never eaten a feijoada in Rio with the same meats. And every time I make *feijoada* it's a new variation depending on where I am and what market I shop at. Any given *feijoada* can include four to six types of meat, but you can use more or less depending on what is available. Sometimes I mix pork and beef; other times I stick to pork. When I am in Rio I try to include *carne seca* (see Glossary, page 196), but in my American kitchen I often skip it because it means a special trip to the Brazilian grocery store.

Risotto de Camarão e Abóbora
PRAWNS AND BUTTERNUT SQUASH RISOTTO

RESTAURANT: Gero
Aníbal de Mendonça
157 - Ipanema

This recipe is inspired by Gero, an Italian restaurant from the Fasano Group that started in São Paulo and opened branches in Rio. The restaurant brings a small slice of Italy to Rio, and this dish features the glory of a creamy risotto mixed with sweetened squash and plump prawns. You can use chicken stock to prepare this recipe, or you can roast the shells from the cleaned prawns in a saucepan with a little bit of olive oil until they turn pink, add water, simmer for 20 minutes and call that your prawn stock.

SERVES 4

6 tablespoons olive oil

454g butternut squash, cut into 1.25cm dice

Sea salt and freshly ground black pepper

Freshly grated nutmeg

Ground cinnamon

1 litre chicken stock or prawn stock (see above)

45g unsalted butter

1 medium onion, chopped

200g Arborio rice

125ml dry white wine

450g raw large prawns, peeled and devined

Heat 2 tablespoons of the oil over a medium heat. Add the squash and cook, stirring frequently with a wooden spoon, for about 15 minutes until tender. Season with salt, pepper, a little nutmeg and a dash of cinnamon and set aside.

Meanwhile, bring the stock to a simmer in a separate medium saucepan and keep it at a simmer.

Melt 15g of the butter in 2 tablespoons of the remaining olive oil in a large, heavy-based saucepan over a medium heat. Add the onion and cook, stirring frequently, for about 2 minutes until softened and translucent. Add the rice and cook, stirring frequently, for about 3 minutes until the grains are shiny and coated with the onion mixture. Add the wine and bring to the boil, then boil for about 2 minutes until the liquid is almost all absorbed.

Slowly add a ladle of simmering stock to the rice and cook, stirring often, until the liquid is absorbed. Adjust the heat to maintain a gentle simmer. Add another ladle and repeat, continuing to add more stock when the previous addition has been completely absorbed. Cook for about 18–20 minutes in total until the rice is tender but still firm to the bite, taking care that the risotto doesn't get too thick. If the rice seems to have absorbed all of the liquid and is still too firm, add another tablespoon or so of stock to achieve the right creamy consistency, and taste, checking for flavour and doneness. Season lightly with salt and pepper.

While you are cooking the rice, prepare the prawns. Heat the remaining 2 tablespoons olive oil in a 30cm frying pan over a medium heat. Season the prawns with salt and pepper, add them to the pan and sauté for about 1 minute on each side until they just start to turn pink. Using a slotted spoon, transfer the prawns to a bowl and cover with foil.

Fold the squash into the rice, then fold in the prawns. Finish with the remaining 30g butter and serve immediately

RESTAURANT: Terzetto
R. Jangadeiros, 28
terzetto.com.br

Tagliatelle com Camarão, Aspargus, e Leite de Côco do Terzetto

TAGLIATELLE WITH PRAWNS, ASPARAGUS AND COCONUT MILK

Pasta with prawns and asparagus is a classic served all over the world – we all know that. But there is nothing common about this dish, a version of which I ate at Terzetto, a traditional Italian restaurant in Rio. The twist – done Brazilian style – is the coconut cream sauce, infusing the prawns and asparagus with a nutty aroma and richness. I like to make my own prawn stock by roasting the shells with an onion, about 2 garlic cloves and a tablespoon of tomato purée, but any chicken or fish stock will do.

SERVES 4

Sea salt

225g dried Italian tagliatelle (or linguine or fettuccine)

225g asparagus, ends trimmed

3 tablespoons extra virgin olive oil

450g raw large prawns, peeled and deveined

Freshly ground black pepper

1 large shallot, very finely chopped

250ml prawn stock from the shells or chicken stock, plus more for tossing pasta (optional)

250ml coconut milk, plus more for tossing pasta (optional)

2 tablespoons Cognac

2 tablespoons chopped fresh chives

Fill a large pan with 4 litres water and bring to the boil over a high heat. Add a large pinch of salt, then add the tagliatelle and stir. Cook, stirring frequently, until the pasta is 2 minutes away from al dente according to the packet instructions. Drain the pasta, saving some of the pasta water just in case.

Fill a bowl with ice and water. Place the asparagus in a steamer basket and season with salt. Add a small amount of water to the base of the steamer basket, enough to cook the asparagus without touching the water. Bring the water to a simmer, cover the pan and steam for about 3 minutes until the stalks are just tender. Remove from the steamer and cool the asparagus in the ice bath for 1 minute. Drain, then cut into 2.5cm pieces and set aside on.

Heat the olive oil in a 30cm frying pan over a medium heat. Season the prawns with salt and pepper, add them to the pan and sauté for about 1 minute on each side until they just start to turn pink. Using a slotted spoon, transfer the prawns to a bowl and cover with foil. Add the shallot to the oil that is left in the pan, reduce the heat to low and cook for about 3 minutes, scraping the browned bits from the base of the pan with a wooden spoon. Add the stock and bring to the boil. Add the coconut milk, bring to the boil again and boil for about 3 minutes until the sauce starts to concentrate, thicken and reduce by half.

Reduce the heat to low and add the pasta, prawns and asparagus, tossing vigorously to coat everything with the sauce. If needed, add a little of the reserved pasta water or stock and some coconut milk to keep the dish creamy. Season with salt and pepper and stir in the Cognac and chives. Transfer to warmed serving bowls and serve immediately.

Escondidinho de Pato com Purê de Aipim

DUCK AND YUCCA SHEPHERD'S PIE

Bazzar, another great restaurant that popped up after I left Rio, opened its doors in 1998. Here I am including my favourite dish on the menu, *escondidinho*, the Brazilian equivalent of shepherd's pie. The name comes from the verb *esconder*, which means 'to hide', referring to the meat hidden under a layer of starch. You can make this recipe in stages; if you have the chance to season the duck the night (or up to 3 days) before, great; if not, not a big deal. The entire pie can be assembled ahead and kept in the fridge for up to 5 days. This recipe elevates the kitchen skills of the home cook, taking carioca home cooking to a level approaching alchemy.

SERVES 8–10

8 whole duck legs, trimmed of excess fat (225g per leg)

Sea salt and freshly ground black pepper

3 tablespoons olive oil, plus extra for oiling

2 carrots, cut into 2.5cm pieces

2 celery sticks, cut into 2.5cm pieces

1 large onion, thickly sliced

2 bay leaves

Freshly grated nutmeg

Pinch of paprika

Pinch of cayenne pepper

125ml dry white wine

1 litre chicken stock

4 bacon rashers, diced

4 garlic cloves, very finely chopped

1 medium onion, finely diced

1 teaspoon dried oregano

4 plum tomatoes, peeled, deseeded and diced

20g fresh parsley, chopped

Position an oven shelf at the bottom position of the oven and preheat the oven to 160°C/Gas Mark 3.

Season the duck with salt and pepper on both sides.

Heat 1 tablespoon of the olive oil in a large, flameproof casserole dish over a medium-high heat. Working in batches, add the duck legs skin side down and brown them for about 4 minutes on each side (you are looking for gorgeously golden crisp skin). The legs will render a lot of fat; have a small bowl nearby and spoon the fat out. Transfer the duck to a bowl and cover with foil to keep it moist.

To the fat that's left in the pan (if there is too much, spoon some out), add the carrots, celery, sliced onion and bay leaves. Season lightly with salt, pepper, nutmeg and the paprika and cayenne. Reduce the heat to medium-low and cook for 6–8 minutes, stirring often with a wooden spoon, until the vegetables are softened.

Add the wine and bring to the boil, scraping with a wooden spoon to release the browned bits from the base of the pan. Cook for about 3 minutes to reduce the wine by half. Add the stock and bring to the boil. Return the duck to the pan; it should be almost covered in broth (if not, add more stock or water). Cover the pan and transfer to the oven. Cook for 1½–2 hours until the duck is very tender, checking often to make sure the liquid is simmering and the liquid level is right – the duck legs should look like alligators at rest in a swamp; if not, add more stock or water.

Remove from the oven and leave to rest for 30 minutes. (At this point you can cool the dish, transfer the duck and sauce to a storage container with a tight-fitting lid and refrigerate for up to 3 days.)

When the duck is cool enough to handle, remove it from the cooking liquid. Strain, reserving the stock and discarding the vegetables (hold on to them to add to the filling if you like). Thinly shred the meat (you should have about 860g) and set aside. Discard the skin and bones or save it for duck stock.

Preheat the oven to 180°C/Gas Mark 4 and then oil a 23cm x 33cm baking dish.

YUCCA TOPPING

3 pieces (about 1 kg) yucca (cassava), peeled and cut into 5cm pieces

Sea salt

175ml double cream

45g unsalted butter, at room temperature

Freshly ground black pepper

225g goat's cheese, crumbled

50g Parmesan cheese, freshly grated

COOKING TIP: My formal culinary training instinct tells me never to pass a tuber vegetable such as potato – or in this case, yucca (also known as manioc or cassava) – through a food mill. But I noticed that many Brazilians run yucca through a blender! So I decided to give it a try, and I have to admit that when working with yucca, it simply doesn't mash as easily as potatoes, so even though it goes against all instincts, using a blender or food processor here comes in handy. (But if this is still against your cooking principals, try using an electric mixer with the paddle attachment; it's the mid-point between a food processor and a food mill, at least regarding yucca.)

Heat the remaining 2 tablespoons olive oil in a large frying pan over a medium heat. Add the bacon and cook, stirring frequently, for about 4 minutes until it just begins to get crisp. Add the garlic and cook for about 1 minute until it just begins to turn golden. Add the diced onion and the oregano, season lightly with salt and pepper and cook for about 2 minutes, adjusting the heat as necessary. Add the tomatoes and cook for 3–4 minutes until they start to break down and release their liquid. Add the shredded duck and stir well. Pour in 500–625ml of the reserved stock – you want to have just enough liquid in the pan to moisten the duck. Taste and season with salt and pepper. (If you saved the vegetables from the braising liquid, cut them into small dice and add them now.) Bring to a simmer and cook for 10 minutes for the flavours to meld. Add the parsley, spread the duck into the prepared baking dish and leave to cool cool.

To make the yucca topping, place the yucca in a large saucepan, add water to cover by about 2.5cm, add a large pinch of salt and bring to the boil over a high heat. Reduce the heat to low and cook for 20–25 minutes until the yucca is tender enough to be pierced easily with the tip of a knife.

Meanwhile, warm the cream in a small saucepan.

Drain the yucca, then place it in the bowl of a food processor. With the machine running, add the hot cream and the butter through the feed tube and process until smooth. Season with salt and pepper.

Spread the yucca over the duck filling, smoothing it evenly with a spatula. Some liquid from the duck might appear – that's okay. Sprinkle with the goat's cheese and Parmesan cheese. Place the pie on a baking sheet to catch any dripping juices and bake for about 30 minutes until hot and bubbly.

Leave to cool for 15 minutes before serving.

RESTAURANT: Bazzar, R. Barão da Torre, 538 Rio de Janeiro bazzar.com.br

PIPOCAO
AMOR
PIPOCAO
AMOR
PIPOCAO
AMOR

Pipoca Doce das Esquinas do Rio

SWEET COCOA POPCORN

João Pereira Ramos Neto is proud to say he is a *pipoqueiro*, a person who sells popcorn. He moved from Paraíba, northeast of Brazil, to Rio to seek a better life, and found it with the *jeitinho*: that singularly Brazilian ability to adapt, be clever and make do with whatever one has. He parks his cart in the corner of Praça Nossa Senhora da Paz in Ipanema and sells popcorn every afternoon. It is fascinating to watch as the line forms and he opens the *saquinho* (little bag) with the scoop. The sound of corn popping is as enticing as the smell, especially for *pipoca doce*, the sweet caramelised version. 'Each grain of corn must be coated with a thin caramel, flavoured with chocolate, and you can't stop churning the pan,' he explains. My love affair with *pipoca doce* dates back to the 1970s when I was a little girl begging my mum, who is also a popcorn addict, for another *saquinho*. To make this recipe, I bought a popcorn popper pan (I got mine at Crate & Barrel) and followed João's advice.

SERVES 4

1 tablespoon Nescau or Nesquik

60g sugar

50ml vegetable oil

75g popcorn kernels

INGREDIENT NOTE:
Nescau is a sweetened cocoa powder created by Nestlé for Brazil, and can be found in any Brazilian store or online. You can substitute Nesquik.

Combine the Nescau, sugar and vegetable oil in a large popcorn popper pan. Place over a medium heat and bring to the boil, stirring frequently with a wooden spoon.

As soon as the mixture starts to bubble, add the popcorn kernels, cover and lock the pan, reduce the heat to low and cook, turning the handle slowly but constantly all the while. After about 4 minutes, the pan will smoke, and the corn will start popping for the last 2 minutes.

Immediately open the lid and pour the popcorn into a large bowl. Cool to room temperature and toss, breaking up any clusters of caramel. In dry conditions, the popcorn will stay crunchy stored in a tightly covered container for up to 2 weeks. If humidity causes it to lose its crunch, reheat in a preheated 150°C/Gas Mark 2 oven for 10 minutes to bring it back to crunchy.

5

COPACABANA & LEME

COPACABANA AND LEME: MUSIC AND FOOD

Another borough, another song. 'Copacabana' is the sound of Rio gone global. It's branded. Who can resist dancing to the rhythm and lyrics of the famous Barry Manilow song? Rio's magical places have the power to inspire musicians and artists from around the world. Indeed, music and passion are always in fashion at the *Copa! Copacabana!*

Copacabana is regal, and many world celebrities stay at the majestic Copacabana Palace Hotel, a landmark that adds plenty of history to the borough. Another king of music, Barry White, wrote 'Rio de Janeiro' possibly while staying at the famous hotel located in Copacabana.

I've spent many New Year's Eves at the Copacabana, one of the greatest shows on earth. The wide and broad dark yellow sands of the Copacabana and Leme neighbourhoods are stage to some of the greatest film, sports and music festivals in Rio.

Copacabana and Leme are also about secrets, surprises and supremacy passed down through generations of cariocas, attracting some of the older and wiser age group, as if only they can exercise on the breezy boardwalk before the sun gets too hot and catch a beautiful whisper of the wind that blows through the bay.

Also bringing a sense of historical style are the galerias, mini plazas uniting commerce at street level with corporate and medical offices cluttered at the entrances. At Galeria Menescal, one of the most traditional plazas in the neighbourhood, you can find the most incredible *esfiha de carne* (savoury pastries) from Baalbeck; see my version on page 57.

This chapter features both traditional carioca recipes and some of my own creations inspired by ingredients I find in Copacabana, like the Chocolate, Brazil Nut and Coconut Cake on page 65. Put on some Brazilian music (among many Brazilian artists, I am addicted to Marisa Monte, my fellow carioca) or Barry Manilow's 'Copacabana' and bring a little Rio into your home with these recipes.

Z-13
PEIXE XICO
PEIXE XICO

Açorda Alantejana

GARLIC AND CORIANDER SOUP WITH POACHED EGGS AND CROUTONS

RESTAURANT: Restaurante Alfaia
R. Inhangá, 30 - Copacabana
restaurantalfaia.com.br

This soup, another dish with a Portuguese influence, is one I can always rely on, as most of the ingredients will already be to hand at my house. I eat this soup at Alfaia, where they make it with water rather than stock, giving the garlic the duty of flavouring the broth, but I find that chicken stock elevates it to a whole new level, making for a rich, full, fragrantly deep soup with a flavour that can only come from a good stock. Then there is the coriander, which is one of the most commonly used herbs in Brazil. If you're not a fan of coriander, you can substitute the same amount of parsley leaves or shredded spring greens.

SERVES 4

90g crustless bread, cut into 1.25cm cubes

60ml, plus 2 tablespoons extra virgin olive oil

Sea salt and freshly ground black pepper

1 teaspoon white wine vinegar

4 medium eggs

3 garlic cloves, very finely chopped

1.2 litres chicken stock

125g fresh coriander leaves

Preheat the oven to 180°C/Gas Mark 4. Place the bread cubes in a medium bowl and drizzle the 2 tablespoons olive oil over them. Season with salt and pepper and toss to coat with the oil. Place in the oven and toast, stirring once halfway through, for about 15 minutes until the bread cubes just begin to become crisp. Remove from the oven and set aside.

Fill a bowl with ice and water. Bring a saucepan of water to a simmer over a medium heat, add the vinegar and mix well. Break each egg into a cup or ramekin and gently transfer the eggs from the bowls into the simmering water, coming as close as you can to the water as you add them. Poach the eggs for about 3 minutes until the whites are set but the yolks remain runny. Using a slotted spoon, remove each egg from the simmering water and transfer to the ice bath for 2–3 minutes. Transfer to a plate lined with kitchen paper and cover loosely with foil.

Heat the remaining 60ml olive oil in a large saucepan over a low heat. Add the garlic and cook for about 3 minutes until it just starts to turn golden and become fragrant. Slowly stir in the chicken stock and season with salt and pepper.

Add the coriander leaves just as you are ready to serve. Divide the toasted bread cubes and eggs between the soup bowls, ladle the soup on top and serve.

Sopa de Castanha do Pará

CREAMY BRAZIL NUT SOUP

STORE: Casas Pedro
R. Barata Ribeiro, 370 -
Copacabana, casaspedro.com.br

The day I went to the speciality food shop Casas Pedro, I bought more Brazil nuts than I knew what to do with. I've read all about the health benefits of Brazil nuts, but I adore *castanha do pará* because eating them brings together all the wonderful elements of a nut and a coconut in a single pod. I often use Brazil nuts for baking, but I also love them in this savoury soup. The coconuty flavours from the Brazil nut makes this warm and creamy soup a revelation.

SERVES 4

205g shelled Brazil nuts

1 litre chicken stock, hot

Sea salt and freshly ground black pepper

30g butter

1 tablespoons extra virgin olive oil

1 onion, chopped

3 garlic cloves

1/8 teaspoon cayenne pepper

½ teaspoon paprika

2 tablespoons plain flour

125ml double cream

Preheat the oven to 160°C/Gas Mark 3. Place the Brazil nuts on a baking sheet, place them in the oven and roast for about 12 minutes until they just start to become aromatic. Transfer to a plate and leave to cool completely. Rub the Brazil nuts between your hands or use a tea towel to peel away the thin brown skin; it should come off quite easily.

Place the Brazil nuts in a food processor and process until completely ground. Add a ladle of the hot stock and season with salt and pepper.

Melt the butter in the olive oil in a medium saucepan over a low heat. Add the onion and cook, stirring occasionally with a wooden spoon, for 3–5 minutes until softened and translucent. Add the garlic and stir, then add the cayenne and paprika. Add the flour and cook, stirring constantly, for about 2 minutes until the flour just begins to foam.

Add the nut mixture and the remaining chicken stock. Season with salt and pepper and bring to a simmer, then cover, and simmer for 5–10 minutes until heated through.

Working in batches, purée the soup in a blender. Return the soup to a saucepan, then place over a low heat, add the cream and bring to a simmer again. Taste and adjust the seasonings, then ladle into warmed soup bowls and serve.

Esfiha do Baalbeck

SAVOURY MIDDLE EASTERN PASTRIES

Cariocas love street food and that may be one of the reasons why we embrace Mediterranean cuisine so well, especially *kibbes* and *esfihas*. At Baalbeck, I don't sit down. There is something about that place that brings my sense of taste to full gear by eating standing up, leaning over the balcony, while talking to my mother and brother about just how delicious everything there tastes. The esfiha at Baalbeck is special; the dough is light, almost crunchy, shaped in a triangle and stuffed with a variety of fillings like ricotta and spinach, chicken or meat. Here I use a meat filling, but do know that you can use this dough with just about any type of filling.

MAKES ABOUT 35

DOUGH

1 sachet (7g) easy-blend dried yeast

60ml warm water

1 teaspoon sugar

75ml extra virgin olive oil, plus extra for oiling and glazing

60ml rapeseed oil

250ml room-temperature water

600g plain flour, sifted, plus extra for dusting

2 teaspoons sea salt

FILLING

450g beef mince

2 garlic cloves, finely chopped

1 small red onion, finely diced

2 spring onions, green parts only, chopped

Sea salt and freshly ground black pepper

2 plum tomatoes, deseeded and diced

Juice of 1 lime

70g pine nuts

1 tablespoon chopped fresh parsley

RESTAURANT: Baalbeck
Av. N. S. de Copacabana, 664, lj 17
(Galeria Menescal)

Prepare the dough. Whisk the yeast with the warm water in a small bowl. Add the sugar and whisk until the sugar and yeast are dissolved. Leave to stand for about 10 minutes until the mixture begins to bubble.

Add the olive oil, rapeseed oil and the room-temperature water to the yeast mixture.

Combine the flour and salt in the bowl of an electric mixer fitted with the hook attachment. Turn the machine to low speed, slowly pour in the yeast mixture and beat for 5 minutes until the dough becomes structured and elastic.

Scrape the dough into an oiled bowl. Press a piece of clingfilm against the dough and leave to rise for about 30 minutes until doubled in size. (At this point you can store the dough in the fridge for up to 2 days; bring to room temperature 30 minutes before using.)

Meanwhile, prepare the filling. Place the mince in a bowl, add the garlic, onion and spring onions and mix well. Season with salt and pepper. Add the tomatoes and lime juice and mix well. Place the filling inside a colander over a bowl, cover loosely with clingfilm and leave to stand for about 30 minutes to drain any juices. Transfer the filling to a bowl and add the pine nuts and parsley. Set aside.

Make the *esfihas*. Scrape the dough out of the bowl onto a floured surface and press into a square about 1.25cm thick. Divide the dough into 4 equal pieces. Cover lightly with clingfilm while you work with one piece at a time. Roll each piece of dough into a log measuring about 25cm long and cut each piece into 8 equal pieces. Turn each piece so that the inside of the log is facing upwards.

Using a rolling pin, roll each piece of dough into a 9cm round (I like to use a 9cm round biscuit cutter to help keep my rounds uniform). Place 1 tablespoon of filling in the centre of each round and brush the edges with water. Fold 2 sides of the round towards the centre, then bring in the third side to close it into a triangle. Pinch to secure the edges. Repeat with the remaining dough and filling. Place on 2 baking sheets lined with baking parchment about 2.5cm apart and leave to rise for 30–60 minutes until risen and puffy.

Meanwhile, set 2 shelves in the centre positions of the oven and preheat the oven to 180°C/Gas Mark 4.

Brush the *esfihas* with olive oil and bake for 16–18 minutes, turning once halfway through, until light golden in colour. Leave to cool for a few minutes on a wire rack and serve warm.

Bilinis de Moqueca de Camarão

MOQUECA BLINIS WITH PRAWNS

RESTAURANT: Le Pré Catalan
v. Atlântica, 4240 - Copacabana
leprecatalan.com.br

The first time I tasted Rolland Villar's cooking, I learned it was foolish to think that only Brazilian chefs can truly understand Brazilian cuisine. Setting base in Rio de Janeiro's Sofitel Hotel, he oversees the cuisine for all Sofitel hotels in South America. Le Pré Catelan, the French-named jewel restaurant of the chain, pays homage to the land that has welcomed Chef Villar with open arms, combining iconic ingredients from Brazilian gastronomy with the sophistication and refinement of French cuisine. Among Villar's many amazing creations are these moqueca blinis. He thickens a classic *moqueca* (fish stew) with a simple flour mixture, then adds baking powder, egg yolks and whisked egg whites. When it meets the frying pan, the flavours of a moqueca in the shape of a blini are an explosion of joy, creativity and Brazil!

MAKES 35

- 90g dried breadcrumbs
- 40g plain flour
- 3 tablespoons *dendê* (palm) oil, plus extra for drizzling
- ½ red pepper, roughly chopped
- ½ green pepper, roughly chopped
- ½ yellow pepper, roughly chopped
- ½ onion, roughly chopped
- 2 garlic cloves, very finely chopped
- 300ml coconut milk
- 1 tablespoon tomato purée
- Sea salt and freshly ground black pepper
- Freshly grated nutmeg
- Pinch of cayenne pepper
- Pinch of paprika, plus extra for sprinkling
- 10g fresh coriander, chopped
- 4 medium eggs, separated
- 1½ teaspoons baking powder
- 30g unsalted butter
- 450g raw prawns, peeled and deveined
- 2 tablespoons olive oil
- Micro greens, to garnish (optional)

Mix the breadcrumbs with the flour in a medium bowl. Set aside.

Heat the *dendê* oil in a large frying pan over a medium heat. Add the peppers and onion and cook, stirring frequently with a wooden spoon, for 5–8 minutes until softened. Add the garlic and cook for a further 2 minutes. Add the coconut milk and tomato purée, reduce the heat to low and cook for about 5 minutes until the mixture starts to thicken. Season with salt, pepper, nutmeg and the cayenne and paprika. Add the coriander and breadcrumb mixture and stir well with a wooden spoon.

Transfer the mixture to a food processor and process for about 3 minutes until completely smooth; at this point it will become a paste.

Scrape the mixture into a large bowl and add the egg yolks, one at a time, mixing well with a rubber spatula after each addition. Add the baking powder and mix well.

Whisk the egg whites in the bowl of an electric mixer fitted with the whisk attachment for about 5 minutes until soft peaks form. Using a rubber spatula, carefully fold the whites into the moqueca mixture. The batter can be frozen in an airtight container for up to 3 months.

Heat a large, non-stick frying pan or griddle pan over a medium heat. Drop a piece of butter the size of a pea into the pan and swirl it around. Pour 2–3 tablespoons of the batter into the pan and cook for about 2 minutes until golden brown on the underside and tiny holes appear on the surface. Turn the blini over and cook for about a further minute until golden on the other side. Transfer to a plate and repeat making blinis with the remaining batter. (You can prepare the blinis ahead of time; keep them stacked and wrapped in foil in the fridge for up to 5 days. To reheat, remove the foil, place the stack in a preheated 180°C/Gas Mark 4 oven and heat for 5 minutes.)

Season the prawns with salt and pepper on both sides. Heat the olive oil in a medium frying pan over a medium heat. Add the prawns and cook for about 1 minute on each side just until they turn pink.

Top the blinis with the prawns. Sprinkle with paprika and a drizzle of *dendê* oil, and scatter over some micro greens to garnish if you like.

Torta de Espinafre
CREAMY CHEESY SPINACH PIE

RESTAURANT: The Bakers
Rua Santa Clara, 86 –
Copacabana, thebakers.com.br

Just a few steps from Avenida Nossa Senhora de Copacabana, the smell of cakes, tarts and *folheados* travels a far distance, even among all the cabs, buses and cars that crowd the section of Rio that houses The Bakers. In this recipe, I departed from the original dough used in *empadão* (a savoury baked double-crusted pie; our version of quiche) by making the whole crust in the food processor using salty crackers. The filling is classic. The Bakers have a spinach *folheado* that is killer, creamy and cheesy at the centre, and I've reproduced that here.

SERVES 4–6

CASE

62 Ritz crackers

75g unsalted butter, melted and cooled

FILLING

450g frozen spinach, thawed

2 bacon rashers, cut into strips

2 tablespoons extra virgin olive oil

2 shallots, finely chopped

500ml full-fat milk

90g butter

55g plain flour

Sea salt and freshly ground pepper

Freshly grated nutmeg

Cayenne pepper

55g grated Gruyere cheese

30g grated Parmesan cheese

Preheat the oven to 180°C/Gas Mark 4.

To make the case, place the crackers in a food processor and grind until evenly crumbled. With the motor still running, slowly drizzle in the melted butter through the feed tube until the crumbs are uniformly moist. Using your hands, press the mixture into a 23cm round, greased baking tin, patting an even layer on the base and all the way up the sides. Bake for 12–14 minutes, then leave to cool on a wire rack.

Put the spinach in a sieve and press out as much liquid as possible, then roughly chop it.

Make the filling. Cook the bacon in the olive oil in a medium frying pan over a medium heat for about 3 minutes until slightly crisp. Add the shallots and cook, stirring occasionally, for about 3 minutes until softened and translucent. Add the spinach and mix until well combined. Remove from the heat.

Bring the milk to a simmer in a small saucepan.

Melt the butter in a medium saucepan over a low heat. Add the flour, mix well with a wooden spoon and cook for about 2 minutes until it starts to foam.

Add the milk to the butter–flour mixture at all once and cook, whisking constantly, for about 3 minutes until smooth. Season with salt, pepper, nutmeg and cayenne.

Off the heat, mix the milk into the spinach mixture, then taste to make sure it's well seasoned. Add the Gruyère cheese. Pour the filling into the cooled case and spread evenly with a spatula. Sprinkle the Parmesan on top. (This can be done up to 2 days ahead of time; cover with clingfilm and refrigerate.)

Place in the oven and bake for about 30 minutes until golden and set. Leave to cool on a wire rack for 15 minutes, then serve with a salad.

Bem Casado

BRAZILIAN SANDWICH COOKIE

Elvira Bona is a Maranhense (a person born in the state of Maranhão) who now lives in Rio de Janeiro, where she bakes up to 5,000 *bem casados* a week from her kitchen in Copacabana and ships them throughout the country.

The literal translation for *bem casado* is 'well married', meaning that one cookie should be perfectly fitted with the other, similar in concept to French macarons. They can be filled with dulce de leche, lemon cream, passion fruit curd, *ovos moles*, chocolate ganache or apricot jam.

Cariocas go wild about the presentation of *bem casado*, and according to Elvira, dressing up the treat requires more work than the preparation itself. The presentation follows the theme of the occasion, from the birth of a baby to weddings and other parties. If you want to dress up your *bem casado*, you may want to visit your favourite craft shop for inspiration.

MAKES ABOUT 25

3 medium eggs

3 medium egg yolks

Pinch of salt

100g sugar

60g cake flour

30g cornflour

SUGAR GLAZE

240g icing sugar

80ml warm water

½ teaspoon vanilla extract

Filling of choice (see below)

INGREDIENT NOTE:
For chocolate ganache, bring 1 cup heavy cream to a simmer, turn off the heat, and add 8 ounces chopped bitter-sweet chocolate; whisk in 4 tablespoons butter and cool.

Preheat the oven to 180°C/Gas Mark 4. Line 2 baking sheets with baking parchment.

Fill a pan large enough to hold the bowl of an electric mixer with a few centimetres of water and bring to a simmer.

Whisk the eggs, egg yolks, salt and sugar together in the electric mixer bowl until combined. Place the bowl over the simmering water without touching the water and whisk constantly for about 2 minutes until the mixture is lukewarm. Transfer the bowl to the mixer fitted with the whisk attachment and beat on high speed for about 10 minutes until the egg mixture is pale, thick and has tripled in volume.

While the machine is running, sift the flour and cornflour into a medium bowl. Once your 10 minutes' mixing time is up, sprinkle one third of the flour mixture over the eggs. Fold in with a rubber spatula, reaching to the base of the bowl in every pass to prevent lumps from forming. Repeat with another third of the flour and then the final third.

Fit a piping bag with a plain round no. 6 piping tube. Pour half of the batter inside and pipe 5cm rounds about 2.5cm apart on the prepared baking sheets. Repeat with the second half of the batter.

Bake for 8–10 minutes until golden brown (any longer and the cookies will get too crunchy). Leave to cool on the baking sheets.

Lay the cookies on a work surface. Elvira likes to scrape the middle of each cookie lightly with a teaspoon (to create even more room for filling), but make your own call. Fill the cookies with about 1 tablespoon of the filling of your choice (I like to use a piping bag for this task) and sandwich them closed.

Make the sugar glaze: Sift the icing sugar into a bowl. Pour in the warm water and whisk well, making sure there are no lumps of sugar. If it's too thin, you can always add more sugar. Whisk in the vanilla.

Using a chocolate fork, drop each *bem casado* into the sugar glaze until it's just coated, then transfer to a wire rack set over a baking sheet. Leave to dry completely – about 1 hour. Be careful when removing the cookies from the rack, as the glaze tends to get caught on the base. Store in an airtight container in a dry place for up to 3 days. For a carioca-style party presentation, wrap each *bem casado* individually in cellophane and crêpe paper and tie it with a beautiful ribbon.

Pão de Mel

CHOCOLATE-COVERED HONEY BREADS WITH DULCE DE LECHE FILLING

If you grew up in Rio, then you certainly know the chocolate store Kopenhagen. You may also know *lingua de gato*, a milk chocolate in the shape of a cat's tongue. How about *nha benta* (see page 176)? Another favourite of mine is *pão de mel*, wrapped individually for each solo indulgence. Many people swear that this tastes like honey, and while honey is a powerful ingredient in the recipe, the reason I love *pão de mel* is for the bigger picture: contrary to what the name indicates (*pão* means bread), there is nothing bready about this treat, a dark and decadent sandwich honey cake filled with dulce de leche and encased in chocolate.

MAKES ABOUT 20

350g plain flour

20g cocoa powder

1 teaspoon bicarbonate of soda

½ teaspoon baking powder

¼ teaspoon salt

1 teaspoon ground cinnamon

¼ teaspoon freshly grated nutmeg

25g ground walnuts

183g honey

2 medium eggs

25g sugar

1 teaspoon vanilla extract

175ml vegetable oil

135ml sweetened condensed milk

250ml full-fat milk

300g dulce de leche

900g dark couverture chocolate, chopped

Position a shelf in the centre of the oven and preheat the oven to 180°C/Gas Mark 4. Coat a 23cm x 33cm baking tin with cooking spray, line the base with baking parchment and spray again.

Sift the flour, cocoa, bicarbonate of soda, baking powder, salt, cinnamon and nutmeg into a large bowl. Add the ground walnuts and mix until well combined.

In another large bowl, whisk together the honey, eggs, sugar, vanilla, vegetable oil, condensed milk and milk.

Pour the liquid ingredients over the flour mixture and fold in with a rubber spatula to form a batter, making sure there are no pockets of flour remaining. Pour the batter into the prepared pan and smooth the top with a spatula. Bake the cake for 35–40 minutes until the top starts to crack and a skewer inserted into the centre comes out clean.

Transfer the cake to a wire rack and leave to cool for 10 minutes. Run a knife around the edges, place another rack on top and invert. Peel the lining paper off and invert again so that the cake rests right side up. Leave to cool completely. (The cake can be wrapped in clingfilm and kept in the fridge for up to 5 days in advance.)

Using a long serrated knife, trim the sides and top of the cake. Slice the cake horizontally in half. I like to slice each half once more, for 4 layers in total. Using a 5.5cm round biscuit cutter, cut out as many rounds as you can from each slice of cake. Discard all the scraps, or make a preview of the finished dessert by spreading some dulce de leche on a piece of scrap and nibble at it. Transfer the rounds of *pão de mel* to a baking sheet and arrange them in pairs, leaving a little space between them. You should have about 40 rounds.

Place 1–2 tablespoons dulce de leche between 2 cake rounds to make a sandwich, pressing down lightly so that the dulce de leche reaches the edges. Repeat until you have sandwiched all the rounds.

Place the chopped chocolate in a heatproof bowl set over a saucepan filled with simmering water (not touching the water) and heat the

RESTAURANT: Kopenhagan
Rua Ataulfo de Paiva, 1025 -
Leblon kopenhagen.com.br

COOKING TIP: I prefer not to use hard chocolate in this recipe, as the cake is too big to manage it (while a bonbon would be just perfect). Instead I use coating chocolate, which doesn't require tempering at all. The truth is that coating chocolate is not pure chocolate; it is mixed with vegetable fat. In the past, many pastry chefs looked at coating chocolate with disdain, but in recent years chocolate brands have improved to the point that if you use a high-quality brand, no one will ever know it is not pure chocolate. I use the Felchlin brand, which comes in *pistoles* (coin-shaped pieces of chocolate), so you don't even need to chop it. Most often I use shop-bought dulce de leche, but you can make your own by cooking a can of sweetened condensed milk in a large sauceapn at a simmer for 4 hours or in a pressure cooker for 1 hour.

chocolate, stirring, until it's just melted. Remove the chocolate from the heat, then drop a *pão de mel* into the chocolate glaze and flip to cover the entire outside. Using a chocolate fork, lift it and allow the excess glaze to drop. Place on a baking sheet covered with baking parchment. Repeat until all the *pão de mel* are covered.

Bolo de Chocolate com Castanha do Pará e Côco

CHOCOLATE, BRAZIL NUT AND COCONUT CAKE

One sunny summer day in Rio, I was visiting Casas Pedro, a store in Copacabana (see box on page 56), where you can easily spend an hour browsing through nuts, spices and condiments. I fell into a chat with the vendor, who told me that a bag of *castanha do pará* (Brazil nuts) had just arrived. By the end of my shopping spree, I had bought a handful of nuts, coconut and a few other Brazilian ingredients. I knew exactly what I wanted to prepare with these treasures: a Brazil nut cake, one that features chocolate prominently. All those nuts were screaming for chocolate, and so was I! This chewy chocolate torte, nicknamed Choco Nut Cake, packs more Brazilian flavour than most chocolate desserts, making it very gratifying to make. One word of caution: it is very important to keep the cake moist; so, just as you would do for a brownie, take care not to overbake it.

SERVES 6–8

Plain flour, for dusting

185g dark chocolate, chopped

170g shelled Brazil nuts

90g unsweetened dessicated coconut

125g unsalted butter, at room temperature, plus extra for greasing

130g sugar

4 medium eggs

1 teaspoon coconut extract or rum

Cocoa powder, to decorate

Preheat the oven to 180°C/Gas Mark 4. Butter a 23cm round cake tin, line the base with baking parchment, butter again and dust with flour.

Place the chocolate in a heatproof bowl set over a saucepan filled with simmering water (not touching the water). Heat until melted, then remove from the heat.

Process the Brazil nuts and coconut in a food processor for about 30 seconds until finely ground. (All nuts release oil when ground, and Brazil nuts contain lots of oil, so be careful not to let the mixture turn into a paste.) Transfer to a bowl.

Using the same food processor bowl, process the butter and sugar until smooth.

With the motor running, add the eggs, one at a time, and the coconut extract or rum and process until smooth, stopping occasionally to scrape the sides of the bowl.

Add the nut mixture and melted chocolate and pulse to blend. Pour the mixture into the prepared cake tin and spread evenly with a spatula.

Bake for 25–28 minutes until the centre is slightly puffed. Transfer to a wire rack to cool for 15 minutes, then invert onto a serving plate, peel the lining paper off and invert again. Leave to cool completely. Sprinkle cocoa all over the cake just before serving.

JARDIM BÔTANICO, GÁVEA & LAGOA

JARDIM BOTÂNICO, GÁVEA, & LAGOA: TROPICAL WONDERS

My mid-1970s childhood in Rio was a tropical wonderland of *pedalinho na lagoa* (pedalling in a swan boat on the lagoon), going to Clube Caiçaras (a club that was practically my second home in Rio), also located at Lagoa and many walking tours through the Jardim Botânico (Rio's botanical garden).

I was comforted by *empadinhas* from Chez Anne (page 72) and often craved fruit ice cream from Mil Frutas (page 81), places I visit often every time I go back. Lunch at Caiçaras was often steak with mustard sauce (page 73) while watching handsome men row on Lagoa Rodrigo de Freitas. It's impossible to live in Rio without looking at its beautiful people, without feeling the joy of being alive, without singing the lyrics of the music, without feeling the heat oozing through your pores. In Rio, life is a party, every day of the year.

Cariocas are obsessed with exercise, and Lagoa Rodrigo de Freitas (a lagoon) is one of the most beautiful places in town to go jogging. Although the reasons behind exercising are usually straightforward and rational – we exercise because we want to stay healthy or lose weight – exercising in Rio becomes more than just that: it's as if your endorphins double from the visual effects of Rio, and the result is a sense of pure happiness, elation and peacefulness. There is even a local slang word for exercising in Rio, called *malhar*.

Jardim Botânico was created by King Dom João VI of Portugal in 1808, initially to grow herbs and spices brought from India. Each time I visit Jardim Botânico, something different captures my attention. The trees are so huge you wonder how many years ago they were planted. One of the main species of tree there is the pau Brazil, which is a huge part of the history of Brazil. It was found all over the coast when the country was first colonised and it is where Brazil got its name. The tall palm trees, also known as Imperial palms, were planted by Dom João in 1809 and today are the main symbol of the garden. Native to Central America and Guyana, these palm trees can reach up to 45 metres in height.

Along my way to adulthood, a certain muted luxury became the hallmark of Jardim Botânico, with more established urban chefs setting down roots. Years ago Chef Claude Troisgros opened a restaurant there, now named Olympe, in honour of his mother. His bass with caramelised bananas (page 78) is the kind of recipe that will impress your guests with zero effort. You also get a sense of this untamed extravaganza at places like Bráz Pizzaria, where cariocas mingle outside the restaurant, particularly on Sunday nights. I love their sausage bread and have included my version in this chapter (page 70).

This section of Rio is very close to my childhood home, and choosing which recipes to feature was quite a challenge. The following recipes are just a sampling of the riches from this beloved neighbourhood of Rio.

Pão de Calabresa da Pizzaria Braz

ROLLED SAUSAGE BREAD WITH ROSEMARY

RESTAURANT: Bráz Pizzaria, R. Maria Angélica, 129 – Jardim Botânico, brazpizzaria.com.br

It wasn't until I left Rio that Bráz Pizzaria came from São Paulo to Jardim Botânico. Now every time I travel home, I run to Bráz Pizzaria to devour *pão de calabresa*, a generous, well-burnished round bread baked inside a ring tin. Even though this may be a classic in Italy, in Rio it is still a novelty. The appeal of this bread is not a mystery to cariocas: we love *linguiça calabresa* any way we can get it – and this bread is all about the sausage. Make sure you use a high-quality brand that you love.

I took a cue for the dough for this bread from my friend Nick Malgieri, and this bread is the absolute best food for sharing with a large crowd. Okay, so you're going to be full before you start eating – who cares? And if you have the chance to visit Bráz Pizzaria, I suggest you order the sausage bread as well as a bunch of different pizzas, because every pizza there is wonderful, especially the ones with Catupiry cream cheese.

SERVES 16

600g plain flour, plus extra for dusting

2½ teaspoons salt

1 sachet (7g) easy-blend dried yeast

400ml warm water

5 tablespoons olive oil

Vegetable oil, for oiling

450g linguiça, cut into 6mm-thick slices

Leaves of 3 sprigs of fresh rosemary, roughly chopped

SPECIAL EQUIPMENT:
2-litre ring tin

Sift the flour and salt into a large bowl.

Whisk the yeast into the warm water in a small bowl and leave to stand for about 5 minutes until bubbling. Whisk in 3 tablespoons of the olive oil.

Using a rubber spatula, make a well in the centre of the flour. Pour in the yeast mixture and, using the spatula, stir in a circular motion, incorporating more flour as you stir. Drop the spatula and use your hands to knead the dough, making sure there are no dry bits of flour at the base of the bowl and the dough is smooth. Transfer the dough to a large oiled bowl. Cover with lightly oiled clingfilm and leave to rise in a warm place for 1–2 hours, depending on the temperature of the room, until doubled in size.

Meanwhile, heat the remaining 2 tablespoons olive oil in a large frying pan over a medium heat. Add the sausage and cook, stirring frequently, for 8–10 minutes until crisp. Drain the sausage onto a plate covered with kitchen paper and leave to cool completely.

Invert the dough onto a floured surface and press it down to deflate. Divide the dough into 3 equal pieces. Working with one piece at a time, roll the dough out into a slightly rounded rectangular shape of about 35cm x 20cm, distribute a third of the sausage over it and sprinkle with a few rosemary leaves. Starting at the far end of the dough, roll it towards you, Swiss-roll style, pinching the edges when you reach the end. Roll out the second piece of dough and spread a second third of the sausage all over, followed by some rosemary leaves. Now, before you continue, place the first rolled piece of dough on top of the second piece of dough, towards the start, and roll it up around the first piece. Repeat with the third piece, placing the previous 2 rolls inside. By the time the 3 pieces of dough are stuffed and rolled, you will have a Swiss-roll shape of about 9cm in diameter. Trim both ends.

Oil a 2-litre ring tin. Fit the dough inside the tin seam side up. (If the length of the dough is longer than that of the tin, you can overlap. If it's shorter, bring the dough back to the work surface and stretch it.) Cover

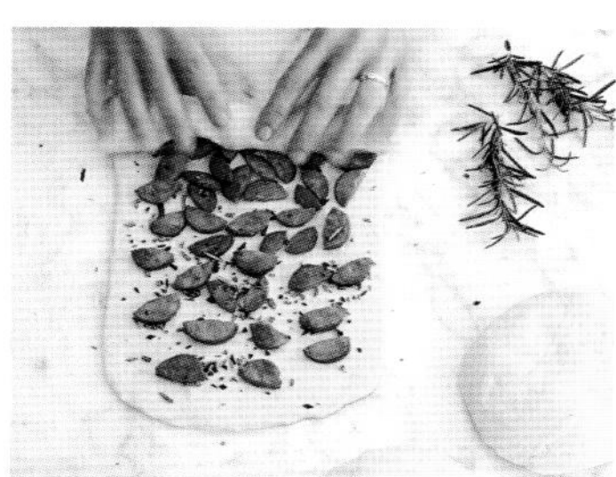

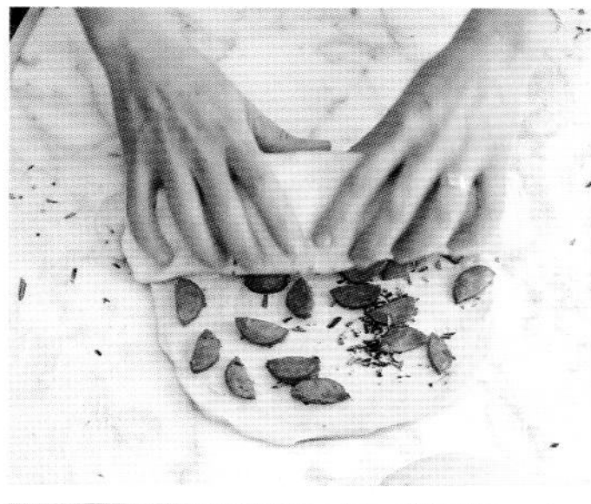

with oiled clingfilm and leave to rise for 1–2 hours until doubled in size (or refrigerate overnight). When risen, the dough will be about 2.5cm above the rim of the tin.

When the dough is almost risen, preheat the oven to 220°C/Gas Mark 7 and set a shelf in the lower third of the oven.

Bake for about 30 minutes until the bread is well risen, golden and firm and the internal temperature is about 93°C. Transfer the tin to a wire rack and leave the bread to cool in the tin for about 10 minutes before unmoulding. Use a serrated knife to cut it into thick slices.

INGREDIENT NOTE: Brazilian linguiça lends itself to slicing better than breaking, but other sausages might work better crumbled. Know your sausage and use your judgement.

Empadinhas de Queijo do Chez Anne

CHEZ ANNE'S CHEESE EMPANADAS

RESTAURANT: Chez Anne
R. Marquês de São Vicente, 52 - Gávea chezanne.com.br

In Rio and throughout Brazil, we love savoury snacks, and *empadinhas de queijo* (cheese empanadas) are among my personal favourites. You will find them in almost every corner of the city, and here I'm sharing an easy version to make at home, inspired by Chez Anne, a famous bakery in Rio. Many empanadas are double-crusted, but this one is single-crusted, making it even easier to prepare, and they reheat quite well, making them a great take-away snack.

MAKES 36

DOUGH

500g plain flour, sifted, plus extra for dusting

2 teaspoons salt

275g chilled unsalted butter, cut into cubes

2 medium egg yolks

3–4 tablespoons cold water

FILLING

450g cottage cheese, drained in a colander overnight

1 tablespoon extra virgin olive oil

1 teaspoon dried oregano

Sea salt and freshly ground black pepper

125ml full-fat milk

125ml double cream

1 medium egg

25g plain flour

28g Parmesan cheese, freshly grated

Freshly grated nutmeg

Pinch of cayenne pepper

Make the dough. Place the flour and salt in the bowl of a food processor. Add the butter and pulse about 20 times to mix it in. Add the egg yolks and pulse again to combine. Add the cold water and pulse until the dough just starts to come together. Place the dough on a floured surface and gather it into a ball, then shape it into a flat disc. Wrap in clingfilm and refrigerate for at least 30 minutes. (This can be done up to 2 days ahead.)

Remove the dough from the fridge at least 20 minutes before rolling so that it becomes malleable. Roll out the dough on a lightly floured surface until 6mm thick, and use a round biscuit cutter slightly larger than the tartlet moulds to cut out rounds. Cut them close together to get as many rounds as possible. Carefully lift each round and fit the dough into the base and up the side of each mould, leaving extra dough above the edge. If the dough cracks or splits as you work, patch the cracks with dough scraps using a wet finger to 'glue' them in place. Place the moulds on a baking sheet and refrigerate while you prepare the filling.

Preheat the oven to 180°C/Gas Mark 4.

For the filling, mix together the cottage cheese, olive oil and oregano in a medium bowl and season with salt and pepper. Set aside.

Combine the milk, cream, egg, flour and Parmesan in a blender and season with salt, pepper, nutmeg and cayenne. Blend until smooth.

Remove the moulds from the fridge. Spoon about 1 teaspoon of the cottage cheese mixture into each mould, then carefully pour the liquid mixture on top to within about 6mm of the top. Bake for about 25 minutes until golden brown, rotating the moulds at least once. Remove from the oven and cool on a wire rack for 5–10 minutes before serving.

INGREDIENT NOTE: In Rio we use the most common Brazilian cheese, Minas cheese, see Glossary, page 196. Seeking to make this recipe with ingredients available outside Brazil, I substituted cottage cheese drained overnight in the fridge for the Minas cheese, and it works perfectly. You can also use ricotta if you like.

SPECIAL EQUIPMENT: 36 x 30ml tartlet moulds, about 5cm in diameter, or mini muffin tins.

Bife com Molho de Mostarda e Cebola

STEAK WITH MUSTARD ONION SAUCE

RESTAURANT: Clube Caiçaras, Av. Epitácio Pessoa, s/n – Lagoa, caicaras.com.br

My brother Jimmy's favourite dish growing up was *bife com molho de mostarda* (beef with mustard sauce), which he'd order at Clube Caiçaras, located in Lagoa, a treasured neighbourhood in Rio. We still visit the club frequently, and now both my kids and I order this dish, which is still served the same way, the sauce drizzled on top of thin slices of steak. While the sauce can be prepared with a variety of proteins, it will really shine when paired with a good-quality, tender meat, one that oozes beef juices when cut to the centre. You can make this recipe using just one of the two mustards, but I like the flavour nuances the combination of coarse and smooth Dijon mustards contributes to the finished dish.

SERVES 4

680g skirt steak, cut into 4 pieces

Sea salt and freshly ground black pepper

30g unsalted butter, plus extra if needed

2 onions, thinly sliced

3 tablespoons smooth Dijon mustard

2 tablespoons coarse Dijon mustard

125ml beef stock or water

125ml double cream

2 tablespoons chopped fresh parsley

Season the meat with salt and pepper on both sides, cover and refrigerate for at least 2 hours or, preferably, overnight. Let it come to room temperature at least 30 minutes before cooking.

Heat a large, heavy frying pan over a medium-high heat, add the butter and swirl the pan around. Sear the steaks on both sides until nice and crusty, lowering the heat as needed, cooking for 2–3 minutes on each side for medium-rare or until they are done to your liking. Transfer to a plate and cover tightly with foil.

Add the onions to the pan and reduce the heat to low. Cook, scraping the browned bits from the pan with a wooden spoon and adding more butter if necessary, for about 5 minutes until the onions are softened and browned from the meat juices.

Add the mustards and stir well. Add the stock, increase the heat to medium and bring to the boil. Reduce the heat to low and add the cream. Bring to a simmer (don't let it boil or the cream will curdle) and simmer for 2–3 minutes until the sauce is thickened and light brown in colour.

Return the meat to the pan and warm it for 2–3 minutes. Divide the meat between warmed plates, spoon the sauce on top and garnish with the parsley.

INGREDIENT NOTE: In Brazil, when you say beef (in Portuguese *bife*), we refer to a piece of cow's meat sliced and thinly pounded, usually cut from the rump or chuck, rather than cow's meat in general. I suggest skirt steak, or you can try flank steak or fillet steak. I like to sear the meat because it creates that gorgeous brown crust with deep flavours, but you can also grill or roast the meat.

Filet Osvaldo Aranha
STEAK WITH FRIED GARLIC

Filet Osvaldo Aranha is a typical dish served in botequims in Rio de Janeiro, named after Osvaldo Aranha (1894–1960), an important politician who accomplished many noble things in his career but is most remembered for this dish and for being a self-declared foodie. This dish is classically served with rice, potatoes and toasted manioc starch, but here I stick to the most exciting part of the dish: the steak with fried garlic. You can use other cuts of beef as well, such as hanger, flank or skirt steak.

SERVES 4

6 garlic cloves

Sea salt and freshly ground black pepper

4 x 115g fillet steaks

2 tablespoons rapeseed oil

60g unsalted butter

1 tablespoon chopped fresh parsley

Peel and crush the garlic with the side of a chef's knife. Sprinkle with a little salt and finely chop it. You should have about 2 tablespoons finely chopped garlic.

Season the beef with salt and pepper on both sides. Heat a large, heavy frying pan over a medium-high heat, add the oil and swirl the pan around. Sear the steaks on all sides until nice and crusty, lowering the heat as needed, cooking for 2–3 minutes on each side for medium-rare or until they are done to your liking.

Meanwhile, melt the butter in a medium frying pan over a low heat. Add the garlic and cook for about 4 minutes until light golden brown, swirling the pan frequently to ensure even browning.

When the steaks are cooked, place each on a serving plate, spoon the garlic butter on top and sprinkle with the parsley. Serve immediately.

Stroganoff de Vitela

BRAZILIAN-STYLE VEAL STROGANOFF

RESTAURANT: Braseiro da Gávea
Praça Santos Dumont, 116 - Gávea
casadagavea.org.br

When I was a teenager living in Rio, one of my favourite places to go on a Monday night was Braseiro da Gávea, in Baixo Gávea, where artists, writers, musicians and just about anybody with an inclination for the bohemian life wandered around. There was a certain *je ne sais quoi* about that night of the week at Braseiro that seemed to draw in the most spectacularly good-looking people in Rio. It was cramped and loud, but that was part of the magic. But that was then; now I like to go to Braseiro – on any given day – for culinary reasons, for example for their Stroganoff.

Beef Stroganoff is one of Russia's greatest dishes; it was named in honour of a member of the Stroganoff family in Russia in the 19th century and became popular around the world with many variations. In Brazil you will find differences in the way the recipe is prepared, but also in the protein used: beef, veal and chicken are the most common. I love veal for its soft slices of tenderloin, but you can also use beef (like Braseiro does) or chicken. My version is not based on a single recipe, but rather a combination of Stroganoffs I've eaten in Rio, and is finished with a mustard-spiked cream sauce. Serve with rice.

SERVES 4

560g veal shoulder, cut into 5–7.5cm-long strips

1 garlic clove, grated

Sea salt and freshly ground black pepper

5 tablespoons olive oil

1 small onion, chopped

3 garlic cloves, chopped

1 tablespoon Dijon mustard

1 tablespoon plain flour

60ml white wine

420ml chicken stock

Freshly grated nutmeg

300ml double cream

2 tablespoons chopped fresh parsley

Place the meat in a medium bowl, then add the grated garlic, season with salt and pepper and toss together. Cover with clingfilm and leave to stand at room temperature for 1 hour (or refrigerate overnight; if refrigerating, bring to room temperature before cooking).

Heat 3 tablespoons of the olive oil in a medium flameproof casserole dish over a medium-high heat and sear the veal (in batches if necessary) for about 5 minutes until browned on all sides. Transfer the meat to a bowl and cover tightly with foil.

Add the remaining 2 tablespoons olive oil and the onion to the casserole, reduce the heat to low and cook for about 3 minutes, scraping any browned bits on the base of the pan. Add the chopped garlic and cook, stirring, for about 1 minute until softened and the onion and garlic mixture is dark brown in colour. Add the mustard and flour and stir well with a wooden spoon.

Pour in the wine, increase the heat to medium and cook until most of the wine is absorbed. Add the stock and bring to the boil. Return the meat to the pan, then lower the heat and season lightly with salt, pepper and nutmeg. Cover and simmer gently for 40 minutes–1 hour until the meat is very tender. Add more stock if necessary – you want to keep it moist.

Uncover the pan and add the cream. Cook over a low heat (don't let it boil or the cream will curdle) for about 10 minutes until the sauce is thickened and lightly browned. Adjust the seasonings and garnish with the parsley.

Quibe de Forno Recheado

BAKED MEAT AND BULGUR PIE

RESTAURANT: Árabe da Gávea
R. Marquês de São Vicente,
52 - Gávea

The influence of Middle Eastern cuisine can be found all over the southeast of Brazil, but my personal attachment to this wonderful cuisine came through my dear friend Tatiana El-Mann, a carioca whose parents emigrated from Lebanon. Tatiana's family cherished the cooking of their birthplace just as much as the language. The conversation in her house was based on the Portuguese language, but animated with tons of Arabic words for which there was simply no translation. Tatiana's mother frequently ordered Middle Eastern foods from Árabe da Gávea, a restaurant located at Shopping da Gávea that specialised in foods from that region. Today I prepare this dish – a Middle Eastern version of meatloaf – in my kitchen as often as I would eat it in Tatiana's house.

SERVE 6–8

185g fine bulgar wheat

250ml water

1 onion, quartered

450g lean beef mince

Sea salt and freshly ground black pepper

Pinch of ground cinnamon

Pinch of freshly grated nutmeg

5 tablespoons olive oil

2 tablespoons cold water

MEAT FILLING

3 tablespoons olive oil

1 large onion, finely chopped

680g beef, veal or lamb mince

Sea salt and freshly ground black pepper

Pinch of ground cinnamon

100g pine nuts, lightly toasted

Place the bulgar wheat in a fine sieve and rinse with warm water to remove any dirt and excess starch. Drain and place in a large bowl. Bring the water to the boil in a small saucepan and pour it over the bulgar. Cover with foil and soak for 45 minutes–1 hour until tripled in size.

Meanwhile, make the meat filling. Heat the olive oil in a large sauté pan over a medium heat. Add the chopped onion and cook for 3–4 minutes until softened. Add the meat mince and cook, stirring with a wooden spoon, for 5–8 minutes until cooked through and a little crisp. Season with salt, pepper and the cinnamon, and stir in the pine nuts. Transfer to a bowl and leave to cool to room temperature.

Finish the bulgar filling. Place the quartered onion in the bowl of a food processor and process until just chopped. Add the beef mince, season with salt and pepper and add the cinnamon and nutmeg. Add the soaked bulgar. With the machine running, add 2 tablespoons of the olive oil and the cold water through the feed tube and process until the meat forms into a smooth paste.

Preheat the oven to 190°C/Gas Mark 5. Grease a 20cm x 28cm baking dish with cooking spray.

Using an angled palette knife, spread half of the meat paste on the base of the baking dish about 6mm thick. Spread the meat filling evenly on top and press it down. Now, if you try to spread the remaining paste on top of the meat in one go, the 2 meats will mix and turn into a big mess. Instead, take small patches of the remaining paste and press it out with the palms of your hands and layer them piece by piece to cover the entire pie.

Using the tip of a paring knife, cut diagonal lines to mark diamond shapes on top of the pie. Brush the remaining 3 tablespoons olive oil over the top and bake for about 40 minutes until the top is crisp and golden brown. Leave to cool for 5 minutes before serving.

COOKING TIP: I like to serve this with a mint and yogurt sauce. Whisk together 125ml natural yogurt, 125ml soured cream, 1 tablespoon Dijon mustard and a few drops of lime juice in a bowl. Add 1 tablespoon finely chopped red onion and 10g chopped fresh mint and season with salt and pepper. A side of tomatoes and cucumbers works nicely as well.

Filet de Cherne com Banana Caramelada e Molho Agridoce de Passas

WILD STRIPED BASS WITH CARAMELISED BANANAS AND SULTANA SAUCE

You've probably heard the term nouvelle cuisine before. Now imagine Brazilian nouvelle cuisine. If you can't, then you must visit Olympe, the restaurant whose chef started it all. Claude Troisgros, son of the legendary chef Jean Pierre Troisgros, landed in Brazil in 1978 after Paul Bocuse asked him if he wanted to spend two years in Brazil. Add 30 years and he is still in Rio. I can't help but think that part of what enables Claude to surprise is that he remains, despite all these years, an immigrant in Rio. With a charming heavily accented Portuguese (which has become his trademark) and his deep knowledge of native Brazilian ingredients, he has changed the culinary culture not only of a city but of a country, inspiring native Brazilian chefs to appreciate their local ingredients. In this dish, one of my favourites of Claude's recipes, the sweetness of the bananas contrasts with the flakiness of the fish, and the rich yet citric sauce is brilliant, typical of Claude. You can also make this recipe with halibut or even a thick tilapia fillet.

SERVES 4

SULTANA SAUCE

170g unsalted butter

3 tablespoons fresh lemon juice

2 tablespoons soy sauce

1 large shallot, very finely chopped

1 garlic clove, very finely chopped

110g sultanas

3 tablespoons chopped fresh coriander

4 firm but not green bananas

30g unsalted butter

4 x 140g skin-on pieces wild striped bass, cut from the thick centre portion

Sea salt and freshly ground pepper

3 tablespoons extra virgin olive oil

Microgreens, to garnish (optional)

First make the sultana sauce. Melt the butter in a medium saucepan over a low heat and cook for about 4 minutes until it develops a light golden brown colour and a nutty aroma. Carefully add the lemon juice, soy sauce, shallot and garlic – it will bubble. Cook, whisking gently, for just 1 minute. Add the sultanas and swirl the pan around. Remove the pan from the heat and set aside.

Peel and cut the bananas in half lengthways. Melt the butter in a large non-stick pan over a medium heat. Add the bananas flat side down and cook for about 2 minutes on each side until lightly caramelised. Remove from the heat and set aside.

Make 2 or 3 small diagonal cuts on the skin of the fish without piercing the flesh and season the fish with salt and pepper on both sides. Heat the olive oil in a large, non-stick frying pan over a medium heat and add the fish skin side down. Depending on the thickness of the fish, it might curve in the pan; if so, use a flat metal spatula to press the skin down. Cook for 3–4 minutes on each side until the fish is cooked through, with the flesh opaque white.

Reheat the sauce gently over a low heat, stirring vigorously. Add the coriander.

To serve, arrange the bananas on each plate, place the fish on top and spoon the sauce around. Garnish with microgreens if you like.

RESTAURANT: Olympe
R. Custódio Serrão, 62 - Lagoa
claudetroisgros.com.br

Frango com Catupiry

CHICKEN WITH CATUPIRY CHEESE SAUCE

Opened in 1934, Bar Lagoa is lit by old-style chandeliers and has dusty floors, wooden tables and white-haired waiters. Talk about old world. But none of our modern amenities matter when I take in the view, admiring the heart-shaped lake in Rio's Zona Sul, eating this dish and remembering the days of my youth when I used to ride the swan paddle across from the bar.

Brazilians love Catupiry cheese. It tastes like butter mixed with fresh cream cheese and a dash of vanilla. While I usually prefer chicken thighs and legs, here Catupiry cheese gives chicken breasts glorious tenderness. Serve this with white rice.

SERVES 2–4

680g boneless, skinless chicken breast halves

Sea salt and freshly ground black pepper

3 tablespoons extra virgin olive oil

½ small onion, finely chopped

3 spring onions, white and green parts, chopped

2 garlic cloves, finely chopped

2 plum tomatoes, peeled, deseeded and chopped

60ml white wine

250ml chicken stock

250g Catupiry cheese or cream cheese

Preheat the oven to 180°C/Gas Mark 4. Lightly grease a 1-litre baking dish with cooking spray.

Season the chicken with salt and pepper. Heat 2 tablespoons of the olive oil in a large sauté pan over a medium heat. Add the chicken, in batches if necessary, and cook, stirring occasionally, for about 4 minutes on each side until lightly browned. Transfer the chicken to a plate and cover with foil to keep moist.

Add the remaining 1 tablespoon olive oil to the pan, add the onion and spring onions and cook, stirring often, for about 5 mintues until softened. Add the garlic and cook for a further minute. Add the tomatoes and cook for about 5 minutes until the vegetables are softened.

Increase the heat to high, add the wine and bring to the boil, scraping the browned bits from the base of the pan.

Add the chicken stock and cook for about 3 minutes until the sauce has thickened a little. Add the cheese and stir to dissolve it in the sauce. Season with salt and pepper.

Cut the chicken crossways into 1.25cm slices and arrange them on the base of the prepared baking dish. Pour in any accumulated chicken juices from the plate. Pour the sauce on top of the chicken and bake for about 15 minutes until hot and bubbling. Remove from the oven and leave to cool for 5 minutes before serving.

RESTAURANT: Bar Lagoa,
Av. Epitácio Pessoa, 1674 – Lagoa
barlagoa.com.br

Sorbet de Cajú

CASHEW FRUIT ICE CREAM

In Rio I've spent many summer nights savouring the bonanza of fruit ice creams at Mil Frutas, which specialises in exotic fruits from Brazil. This sorbet features a flavour dear to my childhood: cashew fruit. A beautiful mixture of red and orange, cashew fruit's delicious taste is quite different from other fruits, displaying a tannin trait, an astringent woody and pucker feel common in black teas, red wines and other unripe fruits. Because of this quality, the fruit is rarely consumed in its raw state. It is mostly sold in pulps, and featured in juices, ice creams, jellies, drinks and confectionery. And then there is the *castanha de cajú* – the cashew nut, of which Brazil is a huge exporter.

MAKES 1 LITRE

¼ teaspoon powdered

1 tablespoon, plus 250ml water

265g sugar

2 tablespoons light corn syrup

2 cups cashew fruit pulp

Few drops of fresh lime or lemon juice

Mix the gelatine with the 1 tablespoon water and leave to soak for 3 –5 minutes.

Meanwhile, place the remaining 250ml water, the sugar and corn syrup in a medium saucepan and bring to the boil. Cook for 3–5 minutes until the sugar is completely dissolved. Remove from the heat and whisk in the gelatine. Leave the syrup to cool at room temperature.

Whisk in the cashew fruit. Taste and adjust the seasoning with the lime or lemon juice. Cover and chill overnight.

Run the mixture through an ice cream machine according to the manufacturer's instructions until it becomes creamy. Use a rubber spatula to scrape the ice cream into a plastic container (take the time to enjoy some now – freshly out of the machine is my favourite time to eat ice cream). Cover with a tight lid and keep in the freezer for up to 1 month.

RESTAURANT: Mil Frutas, R. Jardim Botânico, 585 - Jardim Botânico, milfrutas.com.br

5

FLAMENGO & BOTAFOGO

MODERN CUISINE

This chapter takes us to another lovely neighbourhood of Rio, Flamengo and Botafogo (which also happen to be names of football teams), where restaurants like Nomangue and Irajá are serving up modern cuisine near the Pão de Açúcar, another landmark situated at nearby Urca.

Brazil is changing, and Rio is changing with it, undergoing a revival and reasserting itself. Since I left Rio in 1997, dining in the city has been getting better all the time, with contemporary trends mixing with Brazilian ingredients. Rio is proof that economic growth and prosperity are precursors to a flourishing cuisine, and the current wave of restaurants in this corner of Rio is a perfect example of this progress. Visit Nomangue and you'll taste another twist on *feijoada*. The classic black bean stew is a dish you can find all over Rio; shellfish feijoada (page 89), on the other hand, is a unique variation and among Nomangue's bestselling menu items. At Belmonte, a botequim rooted in this area, hearts of palm soup (page 86) is offered in small bowls before enjoying *petiscos* (finger food). At Irajá the inspiration for cooking hot brigadeiro cake (page 90) is basically the same as making *brigadeiro* itself: it starts with a mixture of sweetened condensed milk and chocolate, then butter, eggs and flour are mixed in. I like to serve it with homemade ginger ice cream, but shop-bought ice cream is also fine. The result is phenomenal and a taste of Rio itself – always hot, very sexy and with a spice for life.

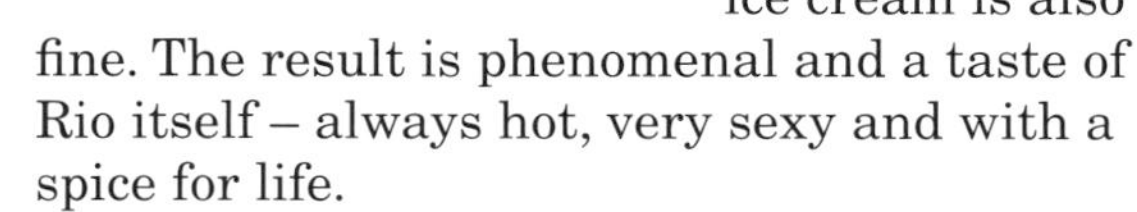

SUGAR LOAF

To have a panoramic view of the city, be sure to visit Pão de Açúcar, another breathtaking landmark of Rio. It is connected with a second mountain, Morro da Urca, by cable cars transporting passengers stunned by Rio's beauty. The monument went up in 1912 and today is visited by over a million people per year. Don't forget your camera!

Crème de Palmito

HEARTS OF PALM SOUP

RESTAURANT: Boteco Belmonte
Praia do Flamengo, 300, Flamengo
botecobelmonte.com.br

This is classic botequim food; you will see it all over the menus in Rio. I particularly enjoy the version served at Boteco Belmonte. You can prepare this recipe using canned or jarred hearts of palm, but it if you can find fresh hearts of palm, it's even better. I love this soup because it's healthy, earthy, creamy (without a lot of actual cream), easy to prepare and simply different. After making it once, I'm sure you'll want to make it often, especially if you have a spare can of hearts of palm in your storecupboard.

SERVES 4

7 x 10cm hearts of palm, or 425g can hearts of palm, drained

30g unsalted butter

1 onion, roughly chopped

Sea salt and freshly ground black pepper

2 tablespoons plain flour

625ml chicken stock

125ml double cream

1 tablespoon chopped fresh chives

Roughly chop 6 of the hearts of palm; slice the remaining heart of palm and reserve it for garnish.

Melt the butter in a medium saucepan over a medium heat and add the onion. Season very lightly with salt and pepper and cook, stirring occasionally with a wooden spoon, for about 3 minutes until the onion starts to soften. Add the hearts of palm and cook for a further 2 minutes. Add the flour and cook, stirring constantly, for about 2 minutes until the flour just starts to lose its flavour. Add the chicken stock and bring to the boil. Season lightly with salt and pepper and reduce the heat. Cover and gently simmer for 10 minutes until the hearts of palm are softened.

Remove the pan from the heat. Working in batches, purée the soup in a blender and return the soup to the pan. Add the cream, whisk well and return to a low heat. Bring to a simmer and simmer for a further 5 minutes (do not let it boil). Adjust the seasonings and divide the soup between bowls. Garnish with the sliced heart of palm and the chives.

Rolinho de Rosbife com Rucula, Parmesao e Azeite de Ervas

ROAST BEEF, ROCKET, AND PARMESAN ROLLS WITH HERBED OLIVE OIL

RESTAURANT: Miam Miam,
R. Gen. Góes Monteiro, 34
miammiam.com.br

This very simple recipe relies on the quality and freshness of its ingredients. It comes from Roberta Ciasca, chef and owner of Miam Miam, a delightful restaurant that serves comfort Brazilian food with a touch of luxe.

SERVES 4

8 thin slices of roast beef (320g in total)

Sea salt and freshly ground black pepper

85g baby rocket

115g chunk Parmesan cheese

HERBED OLIVE OIL

1 teaspoon very finely chopped shallots

½ teaspoon Dijon mustard

Finely grated zest of 1 lime (or lemon)

1 tablespoon fresh lime juice (or lemon juice)

Sea salt and freshly ground black pepper

4 tablespoons extra virgin olive oil, plus more for drizzling

8 sprigs of fresh thyme, leaves picked and chopped

2 tablespoons chopped fresh parsley

2 tablespoons chopped fresh chives

Make the dressing. Combine the shallots, mustard and lime zest and juice in a bowl. Season with salt and pepper and stir. Slowly add the olive oil, whisking constantly to emulsify. Add the herbs and mix well.

Working on a clean chopping board, lay the roast beef slices out separately and season lightly with salt and pepper. Arrange a few rocket leaves inside each slice, drizzle with some olive oil and season again very lightly with salt and pepper.

Shave the Parmesan with a vegetable peeler on top, then roll up each slice tightly.

Arrange the slices on a platter, drizzle the herbed olive oil on top and then serve. Drizzle with all the oil or save some to serve alongside.

Tomatada

PLUM TOMATO AND BREAD SOUP

I love the name of this soup: *tomatada*. Even though it might sound like a late-night fight, tomatada is nothing more salacious than tomato and bread soup, prepared in the Portuguese style. By that I mean *acordas* – bread added to soups and stews (see Açorda Alantejana on page 54). This recipe comes from a Portuguese vendor at the farmers' market Feira da Glória, who told me how his wife makes tomatada at home for their family, and it's one I like to make in summer when I have tons of tomatoes to hand.

SERVES 4

- 90g bread, cut into 1.25cm cubes
- 4 tablespoons extra virgin olive oil
- Sea salt and freshly ground pepper
- 1 teaspoon white wine vinegar
- 4 medium eggs
- ½ red onion, finely chopped
- 1 garlic clove, smashed and finely chopped
- 4 plum tomatoes, peeled, deseeded and roughly chopped
- 1 litre chicken stock
- 75g fresh coriander leaves

Preheat the oven to 180°C/Gas Mark 4. Place the bread cubes in a bowl and drizzle 1 tablespoon of the olive oil on top. Season with salt and pepper and toss together. Spread on a baking sheet and toast in the oven for 5–10 minutes until just beginning to become crisp, mixing once halfway through. Remove from the oven and set aside.

Bring a saucepan of water to a simmer and have a bowl of iced water nearby. Add the vinegar to the simmering water and mix well. Break each egg into a cup or ramekin and gently lower the eggs into the simmering water, coming as close as you can to the water. Poach the eggs for 3–4 minutes until the whites are set but the yolks remain runny. Using a slotted spoon, transfer the eggs one at a time to a plate. Cover loosely with foil or a lid.

Heat the remaining 3 tablespoons olive oil in a large saucepan over a low heat, add the onion and cook for about 3 minutes until softened. Add the garlic, stir and cook for 1 minute. Add the tomatoes and cook, stirring occasionally, for about 2 minutes until they start to soften. Add the chicken stock, stirring with a wooden spoon, and bring to a simmer. Season with salt and pepper. Add the coriander leaves just before serving.

Distribute the cubed bread and eggs between 4 soup bowls, ladle the soup on top and serve.

Abobrinha Frita da Rita

RITA'S FRIED COURGETTES

Rita de Cassia Pereira da Silva is a carioca home cook with several signature recipes in her repertoire. This fried courgette dish is one of them (*carne moída*, page 188, is another). She serves it as a side dish, but I find it to be so irresistibly crunchy and salty that I often eat the whole thing and call it a meal.

SERVES 4

680g courgettes (about 4 medium)

Sea salt and freshly ground black pepper

150g plain flour

470ml vegetable oil, for frying

Trim the top and bottom of the courgettes. Cut them in half, then cut into sticks about 6mm thick and 7.5–10cm long. Place the courgette sticks in a colander set inside a bowl. Sprinkle with salt and set aside for at least 20 minutes but preferably 1 hour for the courgettes to release their liquid. Transfer to a plate lined with a double thickness of kitchen paper and pat dry to remove any remaining moisture.

Meanwhile, pour the oil into a large frying pan and heat over a medium-high heat to 180°C as measured on a deep-fat thermometer.

While the oil is heating, tip the flour into a bowl and season with salt and pepper. Toss the courgette sticks in the flour until they are completely covered. Using your hands, shake the courgettes ever so lightly to remove some of the excess flour. If you shake in a sieve or colander, too much flour will fall off the courgettes – you don't want that. If some of the courgette sticks start to absorb the flour while you're frying, toss the remaining courgettes generously in flour again just before frying.

When the oil is ready, slip half of the courgette sticks into the oil, being careful not to crowd the pan. Fry for about 4 minutes until golden brown and crisp, moving the sticks around occasionally with a slotted spoon. Transfer to a plate covered with kitchen paper. Repeat with the remaining courgettes. Sprinkle with salt and serve immediately.

Vagem com Minas e Castanha do Pará

GREEN BEANS WITH MINAS CHEESE AND BRAZIL NUTS

Summer in Rio is no joke, with temperatures normally in the thirties and sometimes getting up to above 38°C. People are exercising at the beach, the scent of coconut water covers the boardwalk, football is at the Estádio do Maracanã and then more football on television. People are packing their *cangas* (a cloth that serves as a beach towel), their sunglasses and *sandalias havaianas* (our version of flip-flops) and heading straight to the beach. This is my Rio, the perfect time to eat vegetable salads and fresh cheeses with refreshing flavours. I prepared this recipe using green beans I bought at the farmers' market Feira da Glória after a morning at the beach and a juice at a juice bar.

SERVES 4

680g green beans, ends trimmed

Sea salt and freshly ground black pepper

2 tablespoons fresh lime juice

1 teaspoon soy sauce

1 garlic clove, very finely chopped

125ml extra virgin olive oil

70g Minas cheese or feta cheese, crumbled

30g red onion, thinly sliced

40g shelled Brazil nuts

Fill a large bowl with ice and water. Place the green beans in a steamer or a pan fitted with a steaming basket over boiling water. Season with salt, cover the steamer and steam for about 5 minutes until just tender. Transfer the beans to the ice bath for 5 minutes to cool. Remove the green beans from the water using a slotted spoon and spread them on a plate covered with kitchen paper to absorb any extra water. Leave to air-dry for 5 minutes, then place them in a serving bowl.

Whisk together the lime juice, soy sauce, garlic and salt and pepper to taste in a medium bowl. While whisking, slowly add the olive oil until well blended.

Pour enough dressing over to coat lightly (reserve the rest for another use). Add the cheese and red onion and grate the Brazil nuts over the green beans with a Microplane. Taste, adjust the seasonings and serve.

Galinhada

CHICKEN AND CHORIZO OVER JASMINE RICE

RESTAURANT: R. Aprazível, 62 - Santa Teresa, aprazivel.com.br

If you like to see things from up high, you must visit Santa Teresa, a bohemian neighbourhood bordering Cosme Velho, where the divine Cristo is located. The arrival in Santa Teresa is gorgeous, especially if you come through the Arcos da Lapa. The *bondinho* (trolley) is the symbol of the place, and in the centre of Santa Teresa is Largo do Guimarães, where everything happens, where you'll find trendy boutiques, bars and restaurants. From the rustic chic tables of the stylish restaurant Aprazível, your view of Ponte Rio Niterói stretches before your eyes while you enjoy a delicious *galinhada*. There it is served with many side dishes, including beans, plantains and collard greens, but I decided to focus on the *galinhada* alone – in essence, chicken and rice cooked together – for a dish that is easy to prepare at home.

SERVES 6–8

3 garlic cloves, peeled

2 teaspoons sea salt

2 tablespoons fresh lime juice

2 teaspoons dried oregano

1 whole chicken, 1.3–1.8kg, cut into 8 pieces

Freshly ground black pepper

3 tablespoons olive oil

85g Spanish chorizo, cut into 6mm-thick slices

2 onions, diced

3 spring onions, chopped

3 large garlic cloves, finely chopped

2 teaspoons chopped fresh thyme

1 teaspoon paprika

2 fresh bay leaves

450g plum tomatoes, peeled, deseeded and chopped

400g long-grain white rice, preferably jasmine

600ml chicken stock

30g unsalted butter

10g fresh parsley, chopped

Mash the whole garlic cloves to a paste with the salt, then transfer to a large, non-metallic bowl. Stir in the lime juice and oregano. Add the chicken pieces and rub all over with the marinade until well coated. Cover with clingfilm and leave at room temperature for 1 hour.

Spread the chicken over a baking sheet covered with kitchen paper and pat dry. Season with pepper on all sides.

Heat 2 tablespoons of the olive oil in a large, heavy sauté pan over a medium heat. Add the chicken skin side down and cook for about 3 minutes on each side until lightly browned all over. Using a slotted spoon, transfer the chicken to a bowl and cover with foil to keep it moist.

If there is too much fat in the pan, drain a little. If there is a lot of garlic stuck to the pan, deglaze with about 125ml water, scraping the base of the pan, and bring to the boil. Strain into a bowl and set aside.

Heat the remaining 1 tablespoon olive oil in the same pan over a medium heat, add the chorizo and cook for about 2 minutes on each side until lightly browned. Using a slotted spoon, transfer the chorizo to the bowl with the chicken. Cover again.

Keeping the fat that's left in the pan, reduce the heat to low, add the onions and spring onions and cook until softened, stirring occasionally with a wooden spoon and scraping the base of the pan, for about 2 minutes. Add the garlic and cook for a further minute. Add the thyme, paprika, bay leaves and tomatoes and cook for 4–5 minutes until the tomatoes are softened. Add the rice and stir well, making sure every grain is shiny and well mixed into the vegetable mixture. (If you would like to add the deglazing juices from the chicken, now is the time.) Then add the stock and bring to the boil. Reduce the heat to low and add the chicken, sausage and any juice that accumulated in the bowl, arranging it all evenly over the rice. Season with salt and pepper, cover and cook gently for 20–30 minutes until the rice has absorbed all the liquid.

Stir in the butter gently and serve, garnished with the parsley.

Bacalhau de Natas

SALT COD, YOUNG POTATOES, AND PEPPERS WITH BECHAMEL SAUCE

This recipe comes from Manuela Arraes (you can read more about her on page 108). The word *nata* in Portuguese refers to cream of milk, or double cream. In this dish, however, it refers to the creamy béchamel sauce that goes on top of the salt cod. If you would like to keep this dish on the lighter side, skip the béchamel sauce completely, but because the sauce does not really penetrate the fish and vegetable layer; even if you keep the béchamel the outcome will still be on the light side. A glass of white wine is the perfect drink companion.

SERVES 8

820g dried salt cod

600ml cold milk

900g small new potatoes

Sea salt

120ml, plus 3 tablespoons extra virgin olive oil

2 onions, thinly sliced

1 red pepper, cored, deseeded and thinly sliced

1 yellow pepper, cored, deseeded and thinly sliced

1 green pepper, cored, deseeded and thinly sliced

4 garlic cloves, finely chopped

10g fresh parsley, chopped

35g Parmesan cheese, freshly grated

BÉCHAMEL SAUCE

250ml milk, plus 500ml of the poaching milk from the cod

70g unsalted butter

5 tablespoons plain flour

Sea salt and freshly ground black pepper

Freshly grated nutmeg

Pinch of cayenne pepper

Rinse the salt cod in cold water and place inside a large container. Fill with about 9.5 litres water (the volume of water should be 10–15 times the size of the cod). Leave in the fridge to soak overnight, changing the water at least 3 times a day.

Transfer the fish to a medium saucepan (cut the fish if necessary). Cover the fish with the cold milk. Bring to the boil, then reduce the heat to low and cook, covered, for 15–20 minutes until opaque. Turn the heat off and leave the cod to steep in the milk, covered, for at least 20 minutes. Using a slotted spoon, remove the cod, strain the milk and set aside. Flake the fish with your hands into small chunks, or pulse in a food processor for just a few seconds, being careful not to shred it too much (you can keep the shredded cod for up to 12 hours in the fridge before using).

Place the potatoes in a large, heavy-based saucepan and cover with cold water by at least 2.5cm. Add a large pinch of salt and bring to the boil. Reduce the heat to medium and simmer for 12–15 minutes until fork-tender. Drain the potatoes and spread them on a plate. When cool enough to handle, peel and slice the potatoes 6mm thick. Set aside.

Heat the 3 tablespoons olive oil in a large frying pan over a low heat. Add the onions and peppers and cook, stirring occasionally, for 10–15 minutes until softened. Add the garlic and cook for 1 minute. Mix in the shredded cod and parsley, cover and set aside.

Preheat the oven to 180°C/Gas Mark 4 and lightly grease a 23cm x 33cm baking dish with cooking spray.

To make the béchamel sauce, heat the fresh and reserved milk in a medium saucepan over a low heat. Melt the butter in another saucepan over a low heat. Add the flour and cook, stirring constantly with a wooden spoon, until it foams. Pour in the milk and cook, whisking constantly, until the sauce thickens. Taste, as the milk will be salty from the cod, then season with salt, pepper, nutmeg and the cayenne.

Lay half of the potatoes across the prepared baking dish in a single layer. Spread half of the cod mixture on top evenly. Repeat with another layer of potatoes and cod. Drizzle the remaining 120ml olive oil all over and ladle the béchamel sauce on top (the sauce will not penetrate the dish). Sprinkle with the cheese and bake for about 25 minutes until bubbly and golden brown. Serve hot.

Mousse de Maracujá

PASSION FRUIT MOUSSE

It's still dusk in Rio when the men arranging the stands at the farmers' market Feira da Glória arrive with their trucks loaded with fruit. As you enter the neighbourhood you can feel the bright yellow gold light that slants onto each stand, and the passion fruit mirrors that same yellow light for a moment of magic. At Feira da Glória, the passion fruit is loaded with pulp, crowded with black seeds and bursting with wet juices. When I am back home in Rio, I find myself using passion fruit in sauces, salads and ice cream, and generally making it part of my weekly cooking routine. Passion fruit mousse, creamy and tart, fluffy and silky, never leaves my Rio cooking routine, even as other recipes may come and go. When I am not in Rio, I use frozen pulp, and I am plenty satisfied with the results.

SERVES 8–10

2½ teaspoons powdered gelatine

60ml water

400g can sweetened condensed milk

340g passion fruit purée, thawed if frozen

180ml double cream

3 medium egg whites

Pinch of salt

1–2 tablespoons sugar

Stir the gelatine into the water in a small saucepan and set aside for 3–5 minutes.

Meanwhile, combine the sweetened condensed milk and passion fruit purée in a blender and blend until homogeneous.

Warm the gelatine over a low heat (don't boil), pour into the blender with the passion fruit and blend for 1 minute. Transfer to a bowl.

Whip the cream to medium peaks in the bowl of an electric mixer fitted with the whisk attachment. Remove from the mixer and set aside. Clean the mixer bowl and whisk attachment.

Start beating the egg whites with the salt in the cleaned mixer fitted with the whisk attachment at medium speed. As they start to foam, gradually add the sugar, increasing the speed, until soft peaks form.

Using a spatula, carefully fold the whipped cream into the passion fruit mousse, then fold in the whisked egg whites.

Using a ladle or a measuring spoon with a spout, pour the mixture into wine glasses, cover with clingfilm and refrigerate for at least 6 hours before serving.

ALDA MARIA TALAVERA CAMPOS

Alda Maria Talavera Campos is an eighth-generation Portuguese sweet maker, or *doceira*, as we say in Portuguese. She was born in Pelotas, a city in the state of Rio Grande do Sul with a reputation built upon Portuguese sweets. From the time she was a toddler, she remembers nothing but baking and watching her mother and grandmother produce sweets such as compotes, preserved fruit and all kinds of egg yolk-based custards.

Alda got married at a very young age and had three kids, but soon found herself divorced with a family to support all by herself. 'I raised my kids making sweets,' Alda told me. She moved to Porto Alegre (the capital of that state) and had no trouble finding a job as a *doceira*. Years later, Alda met and fell in love with a young carioca musician, who showed her Rio and its major Portuguese influence. She then moved to Rio and opened her store in 2003. Alda's two daughters, Simone and Liliana – the ninth generation – are already in the kitchen helping their mother grow the business. And then there is Laura, Liliana's two-year-old daughter, whose love for baking Portuguese sweets is clearly in her blood.

Ovos Moles de Aveiro
SWEET EGG YOLK CUSTARD

SHOP: Alda Maria Doces Portugueses
R. Alm. Alexandrino, 1116 - Santa
Teresa, aldadoceportugueses.com.br

Alda Maria Doces Portugueses is one of those rare shops that takes you back in time. You feel like you are in a past century with furniture, china and sweets that lived through more than two hundred years of tradition. The proud owner, Alda (read more about her opposite), shared this recipe for *ovos moles de aveiro* with me. As old as the convents of Portugal, ovos moles de aveiro is one of the most iconic sweets of Portuguese cuisine and one of the most popular sweets at the store. It can also be used as a filling for cakes and cookies, but eaten plain – the way Alda serves it – is Portuguese culinary heaven.

SERVES 6

325g sugar

80ml water

12 medium egg yolks

10g unsalted butter

SPECIAL EQUIPMENT:
6–8 x 60g ramekins

Place the sugar and water in a medium saucepan and bring to the boil over a high heat without stirring. Cook for about 3 minutes just until the sugar is dissolved. Remove from the heat and leave to stand, without touching or stirring it, for 15 minutes.

Slowly pour the yolks into the sugar syrup, whisking constantly, scraping every drop of yolk into the syrup. Add the butter and continue to whisk. Now get ready to babysit this custard: cook it over the lowest heat, stirring constantly with a wooden spoon. In the beginning there will be a light foam, then, as the custard thickens, the foam will disappear. Continue to cook the custard for about 10 minutes until thickened (as soon as you see the first bubble, it's time to take it off the heat. Set a fine sieve over a medium bowl. Immediately scrape and push the custard through the sieve. Do not stir the strained custard. Leave it to cool to room temperature without mixing or touching. Don't try to accelerate the chilling process with an ice bath or immediate refrigeration; for a smooth texture, let it cool at room temperature, then chill for at least 6 hours or overnight – still no mixing. (At this point you can keep the custard in a container with a tight-fitting lid for up to 20 days in the fridge.)

Remove the bowl from the fridge. If there is any crystallisation, carefully scrape and discard it. Using a tablespoon, scoop a small mound (about 60g) of custard into each ramekin. Serve slightly chilled or at room temperature.

Rocambole de Laranja

ROULADE WITH ORANGE-CARAMEL SAUCE

Manuela Arraes (or Naná to most cariocas) is a beautiful Portuguese woman who emigrated to Rio de Janeiro when she was 16 years old. She made a life for herself in the pastry business, and today many Brazilians consider her (and her business partner, Monica Soares Verdial) among the best Portuguese bakers in the country. Recently they invited me for a lunch cooked by Naná, with this delicious roulade as dessert. She prefers to use shop-bought fresh orange juice instead of juicing oranges as it has a stronger taste, so I followed her instructions.

SERVES 8–10

12 medium eggs

625g sugar, plus extra for rolling

500 ml shop-bought fresh orange juice

75g plain flour

Finely grated zest of 3 oranges (preferably navel; save the oranges to segment for decoration)

ORANGE–CARAMEL SAUCE

100g sugar

30ml water

250ml fresh orange juice

Preheat the oven to 180°C/Gas Mark 4. Grease a 30cm x 46cm x 5cm Swiss-roll tin or baking tray with butter, line it with baking parchment and grease the parchment. Have a clean tea towel and some sugar handy.

Combine the eggs and sugar in the bowl of an electric mixer. Set the bowl over a pan of simmering water (without touching the water) and heat just until lukewarm to the touch, whisking constantly with a long whisk to prevent curdling. Bring the bowl to the mixer and attach the whisk. Start beating on a low speed, gradually increasing to high, and whisk for 10–12 minutes until thickened, whitened and tripled in volume.

Meanwhile, whisk the orange juice with the flour in a medium bowl, making sure there are no lumps. Add the zest and whisk again.

Using a rubber spatula, in 3 small additions, pour the orange juice mixture into the egg mixture, carefully folding from the bottom up and trying not to deflate it too much. Pour onto the prepared baking tray.

Bake for 25–30 minutes, rotating once halfway through, until puffed, lightly browned and the cake is just starting to pull away from the sides. Transfer the tin to a wire rack and leave to rest for 5–10 minutes. (You want to work with the roulade while it's still warm, or it won't stick.)

Wet the tea towel completely, then twist and wring out the excess water. Stretch the towel out on a clean work surface and dust generously with sugar. Invert the roulade onto the towel, remove the tin and carefully peel off the paper. If the edges are too dark, you might want to trim them slightly, or they will leave a dark trace inside the roulade.

Roll the cake so that the short side is closest to you – be careful as you want to roll tightly without breaking it. Be sure to leave the seam on the underside. Trim the 2 outer sides to make a clean cut. Leave to cool to room temperature, then transfer to a plate using a long spatula.

Meanwhile, make the sauce. Combine the sugar and water in a medium saucepan and cook over a high heat until a light brown caramel forms. Carefully add the orange juice; it will splash. Cook, whisking constantly over a low heat, for 3–5 minutes until well blended. Strain through a fine sieve into a bowl. Serve with the roulade and orange segments on the side.

COOKING TIP: I didn't have to change a thing in the recipe – it adapted perfectly to my American kitchen – but I jazz it up a little by serving it with orange segments and an orange–caramel sauce, whereas Naná serves it plain. You could also serve it with a good orange jam on the side or simply decorated with orange peel.

7

CENTRO, LAPA & ARREDORES

CENTRO, LAPA & ARREDORES: SAMBA & CULINARY TWISTS

Rio is the city of samba. And in this chapter you will find recipes that will make you samba—I promise! It's here, in downtown Rio, that samba is practiced by sambistas and composers and at samba schools. The whole country stops for Carnival, the biggest party on earth. The parade happens downtown, at Avenida Marquês de Sapucaí. In all of Rio, there is no place with the energy of the Sambodromo (the area of samba) during Carnival, where there is a constellation of beautiful women and an explosion of music and dancing. Taking part in Carnival in Rio is one of the most joyful experiences you can have.

Sometimes, all it takes to feel transported to the city of samba is a recipe. A twist over a classic: that's what Kátia Barbosa did when she created feijoada fritters (page 114), a dish that took Brazil by storm. (Another one of Kátia's highlights is the pork ribs with guava sauce, page 122, and polenta turnovers, page 125.)

Downtown has another important identity: it is the business and finance centre, where political and economic decisions are made. I remember the days when I worked in finance in downtown Rio, all dressed up and going for lunches with men in suits. But my favourite part of lunch was the food. I would often suggest restaurant O Navegador just so that I could eat egg white pudding (page 126).

Once in a while business lunches would be held at a botequim. The leg of lamb from Nova Capela (page 119) is a recipe that draws people from all over town, as if the restaurant is fated to do little else, even though everything else is great. Other carioca botequims inspired the recipes in this chapter. Try the Panko-crusted Pork Cutlets based on a dish by botequim Bar Luíz (page 121) or Tapioca Pudding (page 127) when you want a break from the traditional *pudim de leite*.

CARNIVAL

The word 'carnival' comes from the Latin word *carnelevament,* which means 'remove the meat'. Nobody knows for sure the origin of Carnival. Some say that it started in BC as a way to celebrate good harvest times. Around the seventh century, Carnival was made official in Greece to celebrate the god of wine. It was at that time that Carnival started to be associated with alcohol and eroticism, and its popularity grew so much that the church could not contain it and made it official.

Carnival was brought to Brazil during colonisation and was called Entrudo. But only after the Africans introduced their own touch was the Brazilian Carnival born as we know it today. Carnival opened a new industry to music, travel, parties, costumes and commerce.

Of all the Carnivals around the world, none is as grand and euphoric as the one in Rio de Janeiro. This is a well-organised event, and it lasts for four days, starting on a Sunday and ending on Ash Wednesday, when the final samba winner is announced. The samba schools start rehearsing months before Carnival, each representing a particular theme and regulated by strict rules, all dancing for the winning title.

Bolinho de Feijoada do Aconchego Carioca

FEIJOADA FRITTERS WITH SPRING GREENS

Kátia Barbosa, the chef at Aconchego Carioca, an exciting botequim located near Praça da Bandeira, is playing with the most traditional dishes of Brazilian cuisine and creating new classics. If you are a tourist, you might never have heard of the neighbourhood Praça da Bandeira, but trust me, you want to go there. The food being served at Aconchego Carioca is captivating audiences from all over town and fuelling the renaissance of a whole neighbourhood.

I heard a lot about Kátia's famous feijoada fritters, so when I first tried them, I was full of expectations. Well, let me tell you that this *bolinho* (fritter) exceeded them: it is a bright twist on our national dish, one that offers a tiny crunchy taste of our traditional black bean and meat stew. Serve with orange segments and a caipirinha.

MAKES ABOUT 40

450g dried black beans, picked and rinsed

115g *carne seca* (see Glossary, page 197), cut into 1.25cm cubes

115g pork shoulder, cut into 1.25cm cubes

115g bacon, cut into thin strips

1 linguiça (or chorizo), cut into 1.25cm cubes

3 bay leaves

2 litres water

2 tablespoons extra virgin olive oil

5 garlic cloves, very finely chopped

Sea salt and freshly ground black pepper

Pinch of cayenne pepper

Pinch of paprika

Freshly grated nutmeg

185g manioc flour (*farinha de mandioca fina*), plus extra for coating

2 tablespoons sour manioc starch (*povilho azedo*)

Full-fat milk, for coating

1 litre vegetable oil, for deep-frying

Combine the beans, *carne seca*, pork, bacon, linguiça and bay leaves in a pressure cooker. Pour in the water, cover the pan, lock the lid and cook for about 1 hour until the beans are soft and the meat is tender (start at high; when you hear the pressure hissing, bring the heat down to low and start timing). Release the steam/pressure, uncover the pan and leave to cool for 20 minutes. (If you don't have a pressure cooker, put the ingredients in a flameproof casserole dish, cover and simmer for 3 hours until the beans and meat are cooked.)

Transfer everything to a blender and blend until smooth – do this in batches if necessary. At this point the mixture will look like a thick brown paste – not very appealing, but stay with me, it really will taste divine.

Heat the olive oil in a large frying pan over a medium heat, add the garlic and cook for about 2 minutes until just golden. Add the bean and meat paste, reduce the heat to low and cook, stirring with a wooden spoon, for 5–8 minutes until it starts to bubble. Taste (it will be quite seasoned from the meats) and adjust the seasoning with salt and pepper and the cayenne, paprika and nutmeg.

Sprinkle in the manioc flour and cook, stirring with a wooden spoon for about 5 minutes until the bean purée starts to pull from the pan, leaving a skin on the base. Transfer to a bowl and leave to cool slightly.

Sprinkle the sour manioc starch onto a cool work surface and knead the bean paste with the starch until well combined and smooth. Transfer to a large bowl and cover loosely with clingfilm to keep it moist.

Make the spring greens. Heat the olive oil in a separate large frying pan over a medium heat, add the bacon and cook for about 3 minutes until just crisp. Add the garlic and cook for 1 minute just until crispy. Add the blanched greens and toss, stirring constantly, for about 5 minutes until tender. Transfer to a plate and leave to cool to room temperature.

Scoop about 2 tablespoons of the bean paste and roll it into a ball. Using your thumb, press a cavity into the ball, stuff with a small amount of the spring greens mixture and close the ball, pinching to seal. Lightly press the ball between your hands to form it into a patty shape, making sure the filling is completely enclosed. Repeat with the remaining bean paste and greens. (At this point, the feijoada fritters can be covered and refrigerated for up to 2 hours before cooking, or frozen for up to

RESTAURANT: Aconchego Carioca, Rua Barao de Iguatemi, 379 Praça da Bandeira, aconchegocarioca.com.br

SPRING GREENS

1 tablespoon olive oil

225g bacon, finely diced

2 garlic cloves, very finely chopped

1 bunch of spring greens, sliced very thinly and blanched

INGREDIENT NOTE: Just like *feijoada* (page 38), you can use different kinds of meat here. Try to include different flavours, like smoked meats, fresh meats and different sausages.

6 months; freeze in a single layer on a baking parchment-lined baking sheet, then transfer to freezer bags.)

Pour the vegetable oil into a heavy-based saucepan and heat to 180°C, as measured by a deep-fat thermometer. Fry the fritters in batches, adding as many as will fit without touching, turning them occasionally with a long slotted spoon. They will not take on a lot of colour; they will become just a shade darker after frying. Transfer to a plate covered with kitchen paper. Continue working in batches until all are fried. (The fritters can be kept in an airtight container in the fridge and reheated in a 150°C/Gas Mark 2 oven for 5–10 minutes.)

Sopa Leão Veloso

PRAWN, MUSSEL, AND SQUID SOUP WITH SHREDDED WHITE FISH AND FRESH PARSLEY

RESTAURANT: Rio Minho
R. do Ouvidor, 10 - Centro

Minho is the name of a river in Portugal, and *rio* is the word for river; Rio Minho is a fitting name for the oldest restaurant in Rio de Janeiro. Created in 1884 by Portuguese immigrants, one of the specialties is *sopa leão veloso*. This dish was named for a Brazilian minister of international relations, Pedro Leão Veloso Neto (1887–1947), who during his many travels fell in love with bouillabaisse in France. Back in Rio – in those days the capital of Brazil – he handed the recipe to the owners of Rio Minho and asked them to recreate it. But bouillabaisse is a hard word for Brazilians to pronounce, so they renamed the soup *leão veloso*. Today the restaurant is owned by a Spanish chef, Ramon Rodriguez, who adapted the recipe to the carioca palate and to the fish available in Rio. He wakes up every day at the crack of dawn to buy fish especially for this soup, which is not only delicious but also lovely to prepare.

SERVES 6–8

FISH STOCK

2 tablespoons olive oil

Head and bones from 1 whole white-fleshed fish (see below)

1 large onion, quartered

2 garlic cloves, peeled

2 celery sticks, cut into 2.5cm pieces

3 spring onions, white and green parts, cut into 2.5cm pieces

5 fresh parsley stems, cut into long pieces

3 litres water

1 whole white-fleshed fish, such as red snapper or sea bass, 680–900g, gutted, scaled, gills and eyes removed and filleted (head and bones reserved)

Sea salt and freshly ground black pepper

4 tablespoons olive oil

Make the fish stock. Heat the olive oil in a large, flameproof casserole dish over a medium heat. Add the fish head and bones and cook, turning occasionally, for about 4 minutes. Add the onion, garlic, celery, spring oinons and parsley stems and cook for about 3 minutes until the vegetables begin to soften. Pour in the water and bring to the boil, then reduce the heat to low and simmer, uncovered, for 1 hour. Skim off any foam that forms. Strain the stock into a large saucepan and keep warm over a low heat on the back burner. Discard the solids. (The stock may be prepared up to 3 days ahead of time and kept refrigerated.)

Season the fish fillets with salt and pepper on both sides. Heat 2 tablespoons of the olive oil in a large, heavy saucepan over a medium heat. Add the fish and cook for about 3 minutes on each side until opaque. Transfer to a bowl, and when cool enough to handle, finely shred it. Cover with foil and set aside.

Add the remaining 2 tablespoons olive oil and the garlic to the pan and cook for about 3 minutes until lightly browned. Add the onion and bay leaves and cook, stirring frequently, until the onion is softened. Add the tomatoes and cook for about 3 minutes until they just start to release their liquid. Season lightly with salt, pepper and nutmeg and the paprika and cayenne. Add the wine, bring to the boil and cook until reduced by half. Add the squid and cook, stirring, for about 2 minutes until opaque. Pour in all but 500ml of the fish stock and bring to the boil.

Meanwhile, add the mussels to the remaining 500ml stock in the pan. Cover and cook over a medium heat, shaking the pan, for about 3 minutes just until the mussels open. Discard any that do not open. Transfer the mussels to the soup.

Season the prawns and add to the soup, then add the flaked fish. Simmer for about 1 minute until just cooked through. Adjust the seasonings. Ladle into warmed soup bowls and garnish with the parsley.

3 garlic cloves, very finely chopped

1 onion, finely chopped

2 bay leaves

4 plum tomatoes, peeled, deseeded and chopped

Freshly grated nutmeg

Pinch of paprika

Pinch of cayenne pepper

125ml dry white wine

450g medium squid, cut into 1.25 rings (tentacles left whole)

24 live mussels, scrubbed

450g large king prawns, shelled and deveined

Leaves from 5 sprigs of fresh parsley, chopped

COOKING TIP: I find making my own fish stock to be a thing of beauty. Ask your fishmonger to save the fish bones, including a head (eyes and gills removed), for your stock. But if you don't want to go through the trouble of making stock, use prepared fish or prawn stock and skip to step 2. The stock and vegetables can be prepared ahead of time, but the shellfish should be thrown in just before serving. You can also use other shellfish like lobsters, crab and scallops. Use the recipe amounts as a guideline, and have fun!

Cabrito Assado do Nova Capela

ROASTED LEG OF LAMB WITH MINT CHIMICHURRI

RESTAURANT: Nova Capela,
Av. Mem de Sá, 96 - Centro

My father and I are the lamb lovers in our family. One of our favourite dishes is served at Nova Capela, an old-style, pink-tiled botequim located in Centro. There is nothing epicurean about the way they serve this dish; it comes with a simple side of broccoli, rice and roasted potatoes, but the meat is so tender and velvety that it slides off the bone.

A classic prepared leg of lamb is the kind that roasts for the better part of the day, about 7 hours; at Nova Capela it roasts for 4 hours because they use a younger lamb. It's important to trim some of the fat so that the flavours can infuse the meat but to leave a thin layer of fat to protect the meat from drying out and melt slowly as it roasts. The meat is marinated in garlic, onions, bay leaves, pepper and wine for 24 hours.

I decided to tackle this lamb recipe in my own kitchen with American lamb, which has a generous layer of fat, but you can use New Zealand lamb to the same effect. Many American markets sell legs of lamb already rolled and tied, but that doesn't give you a chance to season and marinate the meat properly, so I usually undo the roll, flavour it myself and reroll and tie it again. Feeling a little ambitious, I also prepared a mint chimichurri for this dish.

SERVES 6–8

1 bone-in whole leg of lamb, 2.25–2.75kg

Sea salt and freshly ground black pepper

10 garlic cloves, peeled

4 onions, quartered

6 fresh bay leaves

250ml white wine

250ml extra virgin olive oil

MINT CHIMICHURRI

1 garlic clove, peeled

25g fresh mint leaves

60ml white wine vinegar

125ml extra virgin olive oil

1 teaspoon sea salt

Freshly ground black pepper

Season the lamb generously with salt and pepper all over. Tie the lamb with kitchen string in 2.5cm intervals. Using a paring knife, make 10 deep incisions in the meatiest parts of the lamb, bury the garlic cloves in the incisions and pinch the meat closed around each clove. Place in a large zip-seal freezer bag with the onions, bay leaves, wine and olive oil, seal the bag and marinate for 24 hours in the fridge. Bring the lamb to room temperature for 1 hour before roasting.

Place a shelf in the lower third of the oven and preheat the oven to 230°C/Gas Mark 8.

Place the leg of lamb in a roasting tin and pour the marinade on top; reserve the onion pieces in a bowl. Roast for 30 minutes, then lower the oven temperature to 150°C/Gas Mark 2 and continue roasting, basting every hour, until the meat is pulling away from the bone. After the second hour, scatter the onions around the meat and continue roasting. Check the meat with a fork; it should feel like pulled meat after about 4 hours. If not, return the lamb to the oven and continue to cook until it is.

Remove the lamb from the oven and leave to rest for 20 minutes on a carving board.

Make the chimichurri. Place the garlic, mint and vinegar in a food processor. With the machine running, slowly add the olive oil in a steady stream until well blended. Season with the salt and pepper.

Incorporate the juices from the carving board and roasting tin into the lamb. Carve the lamb from the bone and serve with the chimichurri alongside.

Folheado de Queijo e Presunto

HAM AND CHEESE PUFF PASTRIES

RESTAURANT: Confeitaria Colombo R. Gonçalves Dias, 32 - Centro confeitariacolombo.com.br

Confeitaria Colombo adds a lot of history to Rio's gastronomy. Founded in 1894 at Rua Gonçalves Dias, the bakery displays big mirrors, fancy marble and interesting tiles. It has offered many different things over the years, but those that remain a constant are the *docinhos* and *salgadinhos*. My own memories of Confeitaria Colombo come from when I worked in Centro and stopped by to eat ham and cheese in puff pastry after work. That was the inspiration for this recipe. Here I have kept the approximate size of the *carioca folheado*, but if you want to make these smaller, they make great starters or finger food. Many people buy ham and cheese at the deli counter to make sandwiches, so you might already have these ingredients to hand.

You can also substitute turkey and other types of cheese, but my favourite combination is the classic ham and cheese.

MAKES 4

1 packet (2 sheets) shop-bought ready-rolled puff pastry, thawed if frozen

Plain flour, for dusting

2 tablespoons Dijon mustard

225g deli-thinly sliced Black Forest or other smoked ham

225g deli-thinly sliced cheese, such as provolone or mozzarella

1 egg, lightly beaten, for egg wash

Working with one sheet of pastry at a time (keep the other one in the fridge), place it on a lightly floured work surface and roll out to a 25cm x 35cm rectangle – dust with flour often to prevent the dough from sticking to the surface. Using a pizza cutter, cut the dough into 4 smaller 7cm x 13cm rectangles. Brush away any excess flour.

Using another dry brush, paint 2 rectangles with Dijon mustard, leaving a 2cm border. Fold 2 or 3 slices of ham, one at a time, and arrange them exactly on top of the mustard. Top with 2 slices of cheese, also folded if necessary. Brush the rectangle borders with egg wash. Carefully place the remaining 2 pieces of dough on top, lining and pressing the 2 layers of dough firmly together. Using a fork, pinch the edges to seal tight and use the pizza cutter to trim any excess dough. Repeat the process with the second sheet of puff pastry.

Brush the tops with egg wash and, using a paring knife, cut a small X in the middle to allow the steam to come out. Chill the pastries for at least 30 minutes or overnight (if you leave overnight, make sure you place them in an airtight plastic container).

Preheat the oven to 190°C/Gas Mark 5.

Arrange all 4 pastries on a baking sheet, leaving at least 5cm of space between each, and bake for 20–25 minutes until puffed, crispy and golden brown, rotating once during baking.

Remove from the oven and transfer to a wire rack. Leave to cool for a few minutes before serving.

Bife à Milaneza

PANKO-CRUSTED PORK CUTLETS

RESTAURANT: CBar Luiz
ua da Carioca, 39 - Centro
barluiz.com.br

The number of botequims in Rio makes it the shared-plate capital of Brazil. Bar Luíz carries out this concept as classically as I would expect, allowing me to revisit the past in small titbits whenever I eat there. As a kid, I had no idea that *milaneza* meant a dish prepared in the style of Milan, and I ate *bife à milanesa* quite often in Rio. Today I prefer the dish with pork or veal. This recipe is more of a method than a recipe, and you can use a variety of proteins, such as beef, veal, pork, chicken or fish. It's the breading that really matters. Manioc flour is what most carioca home cooks will use for the crunchy part, but here I use panko (Japanese breadcrumbs), my favourite choice because it yields the crunchiest and most beautiful coating. You can also use ordinary dried breadcrumbs.

SERVES 4

4 thin boneless pork cutlets, about 115g each, pounded very thinly

Sea salt and freshly ground black pepper

80g plain flour

2 medium eggs, lightly beaten

120g panko breadcrumbs

250ml rapeseed oil

Season the meat with salt and pepper on both sides.

Prepare 3 shallow bowls: one for the flour, seasoned with salt and pepper; one for the eggs, lightly seasoned; and one for the panko.

Just before frying, coat each steak in flour, shaking off the excess, then the eggs and finally with the panko, pressing the crumbs in well with your hands.

Pour the rapeseed oil into a large frying pan and heat over a medium heat until it's hot but not smoking. Fry the cutlets 2 at a time for about 2 minutes on each side until the crumbs are golden brown. Transfer to a plate covered with kitchen paper. Repeat with the remaining cutlets and serve immediately.

Costelinha de Porco ao Molho de Goiaba

SLOW-ROASTED PORK RIBS WITH GUAVA SAUCE

When I first visited Aconchego Carioca, I knew the chef had to be someone very special. For a long time I wanted to cook with Kátia Barbosa, and on a recent trip to Rio I was invited into her kitchen. On that unforgettable day, she showed me how to prepare this amazing recipe. Kátia likes to use a guava paste with a creamy consistency, but if you can only find the firm kind, that's fine; just add a few tablespoons of water to help dissolve it. You can also use quince paste as a substitute.

SERVES 4

2 racks of pork spare ribs, about 1.8kg in total

Sea salt and freshly ground black pepper

2 large onions, roughly chopped

6 garlic cloves, crushed

60ml olive oil

4 sprigs of fresh rosemary or thyme

GUAVA SAUCE

2 tablespoons extra virgin olive oil

4 garlic cloves, bashed and roughly chopped

1 large onion, roughly chopped

2 or 3 bay leaves

2 sprigs of fresh rosemary

125ml soy sauce

165g guava paste

RESTAURANT: Aconchego Carioca, Rua Barao de Iguatemi, 379 Praça da Bandeira
aconchegocarioca.com.br

Preheat the oven to 120°C/Gas Mark ½.

Trim any excess fat from the ribs and season with salt and pepper on both sides. Place the rib racks in a large roasting tin, lay the onions and garlic on and around the racks and drizzle with the olive oil. Roast for 4 hours; the first hour uncovered, then add the herbs, cover tightly with foil, and roast for another 3 hours, checking and basting hourly. You can roast the ribs up to 3 days ahead, leave to cool and keep them wrapped in clingfilm in the fridge.

Make the guava sauce. Heat the olive oil in a medium saucepan over a low heat. Add the garlic and cook until it just starts to turn golden. Add the onion, bay leaves and rosemary and cook for about 4 minutes until the onion is softened and translucent.

Add the soy sauce and bring to the boil. Add the guava paste and mix well until dissolved. Simmer the sauce for 5–7 minutes until slightly thickened. Remove the bay leaves and rosemary, transfer the sauce to a food processor and process until smooth. Return the sauce to the pan.

When the pork ribs have roasted for 4 hours, brush with a heavy coating of the guava sauce (use all of the sauce) and return the ribs to the oven for a further 30 minutes, turning every 10 minutes and brushing with sauce after each turn, until the ribs have a rich glaze. Remove the ribs from the oven and cut into 1- or 2-rib portions. (Alternately, if the ribs were cooked ahead of time, cut them into small portions and reheat with the sauce, adding a few drops of water if necessary.)

Pastel de Angú
POLENTA TURNOVER

Regular cornmeal will not work for this recipe; you need to use superfine cornmeal (*farinha de fubá*), preferably the Brazilian brand Yoki. I recommend using thin rubber gloves when kneading the dough, as it's hot and sticky.

MAKES 15

400ml water

1 teaspoon sea salt, plus extra for seasoning

220g superfine cornmeal (*farinha de fubá*)

227g Catupiry cheese or cream cheese

2 tablespoons dried oregano

Freshly ground black pepper

600ml vegetable oil, for frying

Pour the water into a saucepan, add the salt and bring to the boil.

Slowly sprinkle in the cornmeal, whisking constantly until blended. Switch to a wooden spoon and stir, working on and off the heat, until the cornmeal gathers like dough. Touch it – don't worry, the dough won't burn you – and it should have the consistency of modelling clay. If the mixture feels dry, add up to 2 tablespoons water at a time until it forms a cohesive dough.

Turn the dough out onto a large wooden chopping board. Leave to cool for 1 minute, then, while still hot, wear gloves and knead the dough well and into a ball. Cut in half and cover each half with clingfilm.

Mix the cheese with the oregano in a small bowl. Season with salt and pepper.

Have a small bowl of water and a pastry brush nearby. Working with half the dough at a time, press the dough down and roll it out to 6mm thick. Using a 7.5cm round pastry cutter, cut out rounds of dough and cover them with a sheet of clingfilm so that they don't dry out. Working with one dough round at a time, hold a round in your palm and press with your thumb gently, curving the round upwards. Spoon a teaspoon of the filling into the centre of the round, brush the edges lightly with water and fold it in half. Using your fingers, tightly pinch the edges together to seal. This is the tricky part, because as you fold, the centre has a tendency to crack. Patch the dough in the centre if that happens, making sure there are no leaks, though a very light crack on the sides is okay. Don't worry if the half-moon shape doesn't look perfect; it's more important to patch the dough. Arrange the filled turnovers on a baking sheet and cover loosely with clingfilm. Repeat with the remaining dough rounds and filling. (The filled turnovers can be covered and refrigerated for up to 2 hours before cooking, or frozen for up to 6 months; freeze in a single layer on a baking parchment-lined tray, then transfer to freezer bags.)

Pour the vegetable oil into a heavy-based saucepan and heat to 180°C, as measured by a deep-fat thermometer. Fry the turnovers in batches, adding as many as will fit without touching each other and turning them occasionally with a long slotted spoon, for 4 minutes – they will not take on a lot of colour, just darken slightly (don't cook much longer or the cheese could pop out). Transfer to a plate covered with kitchen paper. Continue working in batches until all the turnovers are fried. Serve with the pork ribs (page 122).

Pudim de Claras com Baba de Moça

EGG WHITE PUDDING WITH COCONUT CREAM SAUCE

RESTAURANT: O Navegador, Av. Rio Branco, 180/6 andar, Clube Naval
onavegador.com.br

When I lived in Rio, I worked in an investment bank located in Centro. We had business lunches at O Navegador, and I always swooned over the *pudim de claras*. Traditionally, it's served with the coconut cream sauce that I'm including here, but you can also serve it with berries or a berry sauce. After all this time, the restaurant is more alive than ever, and its chef (for the past 30 years), Tereza Corcão, is gaining recognition for her work. She is one of the leaders of carioca new gastronomy, combining elaborate technique with local ingredients.

SERVES 6–8

440g sugar

60ml water

6 medium egg whites, at room temperature

1/8 teaspoon salt

1 teaspoon vanilla extract

½ teaspoon fresh lime juice

COCONUT CREAM SAUCE

135g unsalted butter

100g sugar

125ml coconut milk (preferably a Brazilian brand like Sococo)

8 medium egg yolks

SPECIAL EQUIPMENT:
2-litre ring tin

Combine 220g of the sugar and the water in a very clean heavy-based saucepan. Cook over a high heat without stirring for about 5 minutes until it forms a light amber-coloured caramel. Pour the caramel into the ring tin and swirl it around, making sure the caramel evenly covers the whole base of the pan. Set aside.

Preheat the oven to 120°C/Gas Mark ½.

Place the egg whites in the bowl of an electric mixer (make sure it's spotlessly clean) fitted with the whisk attachment. Start beating at medium speed until the eggs start foaming, rising and turning opaque. Gradually add the remaining 220g sugar, dissolving it into the egg whites. Increase the speed to high and beat for 5–8 minutes until the meringue is firm and glossy.

Add the vanilla and lime juice. Carefully transfer the meringue to the prepared tin, using a spatula to spread evenly inside the tin. Place the ring tin in a roasting tin. Pour hot water into the roasting tin to come halfway up the sides of the roasting tin. Carefully transfer to the oven and bake for about 1 hour 15 minutes until the top is very lightly browned.

Meanwhile, make the coconut cream sauce. Combine the butter, sugar and coconut milk in a medium saucepan. Place over a medium heat and cook until the sugar dissolves, the butter melts and the mixture starts to bubble slightly.

Beat the egg yolks in a medium bowl.

Slowly pour half of the hot coconut mixture over the yolks, whisking as you pour, to temper the yolks. Return everything to the saucepan and cook over a low heat, stirring constantly, for 10–15 minutes until it thickens to a curd consistency.

Strain through a fine sieve into a medium bowl and leave to cool to room temperature. (You can prepare the sauce up to 3 days ahead of time and keep in a tightly sealed container in the fridge.)

Turn the oven off, open the oven door and keep the ring tin and roasting tin inside the oven for a further 10 minutes to prevent a shock of temperature. Transfer the ring tin to a wire rack to cool completely. Run a knife around the ring tin and invert onto a cake platter. Let the caramel drip for a few minutes, then lift the tin off. Serve cold or at room temperature, with the coconut cream sauce on the side. To store, cover loosely with clingfilm in the fridge for up to 2 days.

Pudim de Tapioca

TAPIOCA PUDDING WITH COCONUT CARAMEL SAUCE

This dessert came to Rio from the kitchens of Rodrigo Oliveira, an extremely talented chef based in São Paulo. Like many other desserts, it didn't take too long to spread across Rio. I got inspired to try it when visiting Feira São Cristovão, a flea market in Centro specialising in foods from the northeast region of Brazil. As a carioca, I love all kinds of pudding, and I especially love the humble tapioca, which offers an irresistibly fluffy and chewy consistency. Rodrigo serves this dessert with a coconut caramel sauce and toasted coconut. These are great complements to the pudding, but even served plain it still tastes amazing.

SERVES 8

95g granulated tapioca (or small pearl tapioca)

375ml double cream

200ml coconut milk

215g sugar

80ml water

2 medium eggs

2 medium egg yolks

125ml full-fat milk

397g can sweetened condensed milk

1 teaspoon vanilla extract

COCONUT CARAMEL SAUCE

430g sugar

200ml coconut milk

80ml water

115g unsweetened desiccated coconut

SPECIAL EQUIPMENT:
2-litre ring tin

Place the tapioca in a medium bowl and pour the cream and coconut milk over it. Cover with clingfilm and leave to stand for 2 hours at room temperature or overnight in the fridge.

Combine the sugar and water in a clean heavy-based saucepan and cook over a high heat without stirring for about 5 minutes until it turns into an amber-coloured caramel. Pour the caramel into the ring tin, making sure it coats the whole base of the tin evenly.

Preheat the oven to 180°C°/Gas Mark 4.

Beat the eggs, yolks, milk, sweetened condensed milk and vanilla in a large bowl. Strain through a sieve into the tapioca and mix gently with a rubber spatula. Carefully pour into the prepared caramel pan. Transfer to a large roasting tin and fill the roasting tin with hot tap water to come halfway up the sides of the roasting tin. Transfer the roasting tin to the centre of the oven and bake for 45–55 minutes until the pudding is thick but still wobbles in the centre.

Meanwhile, make the coconut caramel sauce. Place the sugar in a medium saucepan and cook over a high heat until it turns amber in colour. Add the coconut milk and water and cook for about 5 minutes until it thickens.

Spread the coconut onto a baking sheet and bake, turning frequently to prevent burning, for about 4 minutes until lightly browned. Leave to cool.

Transfer the ring tin to a wire rack and leave to cool to room temperature, then refrigerate for at least 4 hours or overnight. It's important to invert the pudding only after it is chilled completely, otherwise it might break.

When ready to serve, run a smooth knife around the inside of the ring tin. Place a large rimmed serving platter on top of the tin and, holding it together with both hands, quickly invert the pudding onto the platter. Allow the caramel to run down before lifting up the tin. Drizzle some of the coconut caramel sauce around it and decorate with the toasted coconut.

8

BARRA DA TIJUCA

BARRA: THE FUTURE

As a child growing up in Rio, I saw Barra da Tijuca go from deserted to one of the most developed neighbourhoods in town.

To enter Barra, you have to drive through Rocinha, the largest *favela* (shanty town) of Brazil. I grew up just a few minutes away, but I never connected with this world – so close to my own home yet so far away from the world I grew up in. Until the day I decided to visit, when my whole perspective of Rio changed.

I expected that our societies would have nothing to do with each other, but in Rio links between different people are made every day, at every moment, through sun and landscape, music and sports, but most importantly through food. Food can be a class divider, but in Rio it is a class connector, a common ground, an equaliser – through flavour.

The same *feijoada* (page 38) that is served at gorgeous hotels is also served in Rocinha. The same *bolinho de bacalhau* (salt cod fritters, page 20) that are served in the cool botequims in the trendy neighbourhoods of Ipanema and Leblon are also served here as well, on the way to Barra, or in any other favela in Rio.

Two worlds facing each other: look to the right and you'll see the most magnificent view of Rio; look to the left and you'll see Rocinha, also magnificent in its own way.

Barra is the future. The neighbourhood is being transformed to host the 2016 Olympic Games to become the home of the Olympic village. Nearly half of the sports competitions will take place at Barra, where construction of a new street called Rua Carioca Entertainment Boulevard and a private Olympic beach exclusive for the athletes are in the works.

Today this road to improvement, with more than 30 shopping malls, countless *churrascarias* (steakhouses) and many botequims, is just four years away, and that's our reality. High, low, rich, poor, Rio's geographical structure, its gorgeous sunny climate – and the food – bring our population together, always outdoors and beyond the social patterns that separate most populations of big cities by class, race or occupation.

The difference between now and when I grew up in Rio is that the culture that springs from neighbourhoods traditionally marginalised by society is now being integrated with the rest of the city, and cariocas of all classes go to the favelas not just as tourists but to participate in our home-grown culture, trying local dishes, bars and dance spots. I left Rocinha favela feeling hopeful for the future and proud of being a carioca.

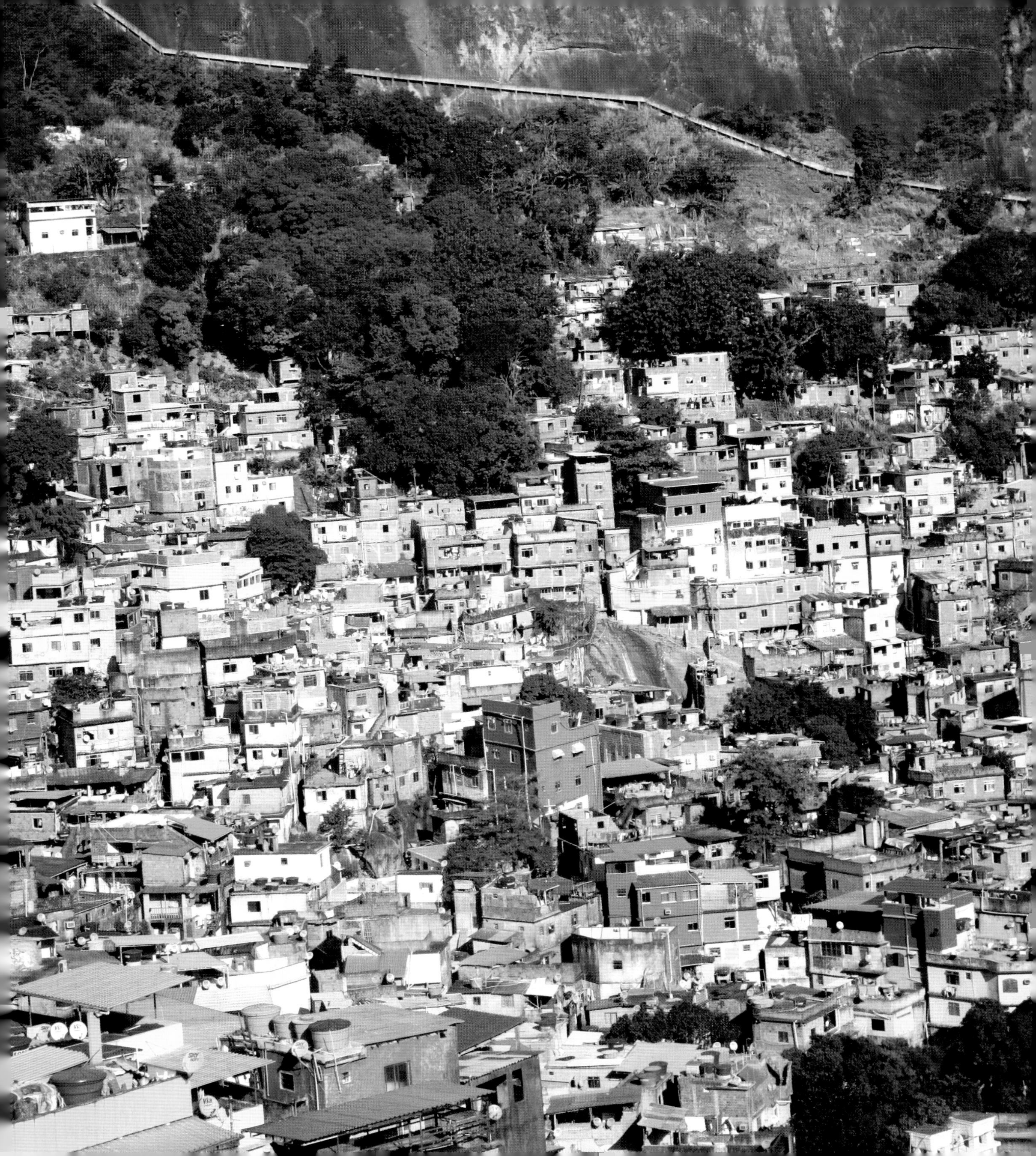
SKY
SKY
Via

Suco de Frutas Vermelhas

RED BERRY FRUIT JUICE

RESTAURANT: Big Polis
Av. Ataulfo de Paiva, 505 -
Rio de Janeiro

Each beach in Rio is a world unto itself; Barra's beaches stretch further than other neighbourhoods', with many juice bars right across from the beach. Big Polis is a classic chain in Rio with branches all over town, including one in Barra. One of my favourite juices at Big Polis is the *suco de frutas vermelhas*, which is prepared with red fruits such as strawberries, raspberries, blackberries and açaí. When I moved to the USA, I found very little to satisfy my craving, so I make my own juice every day of the week using cherries, blueberries or blackberries. Like mother, like daughter, mine is as addicted to these healthy concoctions as I am, and she likes to prepare this particular one for breakfast every morning.

SERVES 1

80g strawberries

60g raspberries

60g blueberries, cherries or blackberries

250ml water

3 tablespoons sugar

Combine all the ingredients in a blender and blend for about 3 minutes until very smooth.

Pour into a tall glass and serve immediately.

Aipim Frito

YUCCA FRIES

I love yucca. I call it the miracle vegetable of Brazil, because it has been providing food for generations of native Brazilians, Africans and Portuguese, and is used in an infinite number of recipes in many forms, including starches, flours and juices. This vegetable is now available from some major supermarkets and is very easy to prepare. Depending on the quality of the yucca, boiling and frying times might vary. In Rio, *aipim frito* is often served as a side dish by itself. You can also serve it as a snack with a spicy mayonnaise sauce made by flavouring mayonnaise with crushed garlic, chopped coriander and parsley, lime juice and salt and pepper.

SERVES 4–6

900g (about 2) yucca (cassava)

Sea salt

700ml vegetable oil, for frying

Peel the yucca and cut it into 6cm sections. Wash well to remove any dirt, and cut it into 8mm-thick sticks.

Place the yucca in a large saucepan and add cold water to cover completely. Add a good pinch of salt and bring to the boil over a high heat. Reduce the heat to medium-low and cook gently for about 20 minutes until almost translucent and a knife inserted comes out easily. Using a slotted spoon, transfer to a baking sheet covered with kitchen paper, spreading the yucca in one layer. Leave to dry and cool to room temperature. Using a paring knife, remove the woody fibres from the yucca.

Pour the vegetable oil into a heavy-based saucepan and heat it to 180°C, as measured by a deep-fat thermometer. Working in batches, slip the yucca into the oil, turning occasionally, and fry for 5–7 minutes per batch until light golden brown. Remove with a slotted spoon and place on a baking sheet lined with kitchen paper; season with salt immediately as the fries come out of the oil.

INGREDIENT NOTE: This tuber vegetable goes by many different names: yucca, cassava, manioc and in Portuguese *aipim, mandioca* and *macaxeira*. I know of no other vegetable with that many names. For the sake of consistency, let's call it yucca in English and *aipim* in Portuguese. Yucca has a woody fibre in the centre, and the older the yucca gets, the tougher this fibre is. You can remove it before boiling, or afterwards (which I find is easier, as you'll see in the recipe).

Sanduiche Natural de Galinha com Cenoura

CHICKEN SALAD WITH CARROTS AND CHIVES ON WHOLEMEAL

This sandwich is a benchmark of Rio's beaches, and I grew up eating it. We'll never know which beach vendor started selling these by yelling '*Oooooolha o sanduiche natural!*' ('Look! It's the natural sandwich!'), but it certainly was a good marketing strategy. The word 'natural' must have come from using wholemeal bread instead of white bread, but what really matters is that these sandwiches are delicious! It's a sandwich that lives inside of me, a sandwich that connects me with Rio every time I sit down to lunch on one.

You can roast the chicken or use shop-bought rotisserie chicken, and make sure you use shredded chicken rather than cubed chicken to give the sandwich the right texture. Herbs aren't traditionally used in Rio, but I like how chives complement the flavours of the sandwich (parsley works too), so I include them in mine. In Rio the sandwich is served ready-made and wrapped in clingfilm. As it sits, the juicy mixture and all its tasty flavours permeate the bread in a soggy, blissful way, making it a perfect sandwich to pack and go.

MAKES 4

3 tablespoons raisins or sultanas

2 medium (132g) carrots

200g cooked chicken, finely shredded

120ml mayonnaise

2 tablespoons chopped fresh chives

Sea salt and freshly ground black pepper

8 slices wholemeal bread

Plump the raisins by soaking them in 125ml warm water for 5 minutes.

Meanwhile, grate the carrots on the largest holes of a box grater. Place the grated carrot in a bowl.

Drain the raisins and add them to the bowl with the chicken, mayonnaise and chives. Season with salt and pepper and mix the ingredients with a rubber spatula.

Divide the mixture between the slices of bread and then sandwich them together.

Bacalhau à Lagareira

FRESH COD WITH ONIONS, GARLIC, POTATOES, AND TENDERSTEM BROCCOLI

RESTAURANT: Adegão Português, R. Shopping Rio Design Barra, Av das Americas, 7.777, 3° piso, Barra da Tijuca, adegaoportugues.com.br

Lagareiro is the Portuguese word for a person who owns an olive oil press, and indeed, olive oil is an important ingredient in this recipe. This recipe is incredibly simple, yet it delivers flavours in a brilliant way. At the restaurant Adegão Português, the recipe is prepared using salt cod, but here I make it with fresh cod since it is widely available in the United States. Every time I make this dish, without fail I am asked for the recipe. It is healthy and very easy to put together—everything can be prepared ahead of time and refrigerated for up to 2 days, with the dish assembled just before baking.

SERVES 4

680g small new potatoes

Sea salt

450g tenderstem broccoli, thick lower stalks removed

6 tablespoons extra virgin olive oil

2 onions, thinly sliced

4 garlic cloves, very finely chopped

570g skinless cod fillet, cut into 4 equal pieces

60ml white wine, water or fish stock

Freshly ground black pepper

Place the potatoes in a large, heavy-based saucepan and cover with cold water by at least 2.5cm. Add a large pinch of salt and bring to the boil. Reduce the heat to medium and simmer for 12–15 minutes until the potatoes are fork-tender. Drain in a colander and spread onto a plate. When cool enough to handle, peel and quarter the potatoes. Set aside in a bowl.

Preheat the oven to 180°C/Gas Mark 4. Lightly coat a large, shallow baking dish with cooking spray.

Place the broccoli in a steamer or a pan fitted with a steaming basket over simmering water. Season with salt, cover the pan and steam for about 5 minutes until the stalks are just tender. Transfer the broccoli to a plate and set aside.

Heat 2 tablespoons of the olive oil in a large frying pan over a low heat, add the onions and cook, stirring occasionally with a wooden spoon, for about 10 minutes until softened and translucent. (Resist the temptation to turn the heat to high, or the onions will brown; the slower you cook the onions, the sweeter they get.) Transfer to the bowl with the potatoes and toss together; season lightly with salt and pepper.

Heat 1 tablespoon of the remaining olive oil in a small frying pan over a low heat. Add the garlic and cook for 1–2 minutes until it just starts to turn golden. Immediately transfer to a plate lined with a double thickness of kitchen paper.

Arrange the potato–onion mixture on the base of the baking dish and place the broccoli on top.

Season the cod with salt and pepper and arrange on top of the vegetables. Sprinkle the garlic on top, drizzle the remaining 3 tablespoons olive oil all over and bake for 12–15 minutes until the fish is just cooked.

Remove the baking dish from the oven; spoon the cod onto warm plates and serve immediately.

Purê de Abóbora com Carne Seca

PULLED CARNE SECA WITH BUTTERNUT SQUASH PUREE

RESTAURANT: Devassa, Rua Sen Vergueiro 2, Rio de Janeiro
devassa.com.br

Carne seca, a dried and salt-cured meat, is a huge part of Brazilian cooking. It comes from a lean cut such as top round, because too much marbled fat (what gives that buttery richness we want in our cooked meats) makes the dried meat too tough. This dish is a botequim-inspired delicacy, like one I've had at Devassa, a botequim in Barra.

SERVES 6

1kg *carne seca*

3 tablespoons extra virgin olive oil

2 large onions, thinly sliced

Sea salt and freshly ground black pepper

10g chopped fresh parsley

2 tablespoons olive oil

1 butternut squash, peeled, deseeded and diced

Pinch of freshly grated nutmeg

Pinch of ground cinnamon

Pinch of sugar

30g unsalted butter

COOKING TIP: This recipe calls for advance planning, as it requires reconstituting the meat by soaking it in cold water overnight. Brazilians like to use a pressure cooker for everything, so we often use one for *carne seca* to make it tender, but braising is a perfect alternative. This can be done up to 2 days ahead of time; keep the meat in the braising liquid. If you cannot find carne seca, substitute a strong-flavoured smoked meat or brisket. As long as you use some sort of pulled meat that's full of flavour, this dish will taste delicious.

Rinse the *carne seca* in cold water and place it inside a large container. Cover with cold water, cover the container and place in the fridge for 12–24 hours, changing the water at least 3 times.

Drain the meat and place in a saucepan, fill with water to cover halfway, then cover the pan, bring to a simmer and cook over a low heat for at least 3 hours until the meat is tender. Alternatively, cook in a pressure cooker for 45 minutes after the pressure starts.

Remove the meat from the pan and discard the water. When the meat is cool enough to handle, thinly shred it, discarding the fat and any undesired grisly parts. You should have about 350g meat.

Heat the extra virgin olive oil in a large frying pan over a medium heat and add the onions. Cook, stirring frequently with a wooden spoon, for about 10 minutes until softened. If the onions start to get some colour, add 1–2 tablespoons water. Add the pulled meat, season with pepper and sprinkle with the parsley.

Heat the olive oil in a medium saucepan over a medium heat. Add the pumpkin and cook, stirring frequently with a wooden spoon, for 5 minutes. Partially cover the pan and cook for a further 15–20 minutes until the squash is tender, checking frequently to make sure it doesn't brown (if it does, add about 60ml water). Season with salt and pepper and add the nutmeg, cinnamon and sugar. Add the butter and stir well.

Transfer to a food processor and purée the pumpkin until smooth.

Arrange the purée on an oval platter, spoon the pulled meat mixture on top and serve immediately.

9

BÚZIOS

A TRIP TO BÚZIOS

Búzios is one of Brazil's best beach resorts, and a mere three hours from Rio by car. The map of Búzios is a peninsula clipped with many small bays (over twenty), each one hosting a breathtaking beach.

Originally settled by European smugglers of pau Brazil wood and slave traders during the seventeenth century, this region prospered and became a picturesque fishing village. It was only in the 1960s, however, that the region found more notoriety after Brigitte Bardot, the famous French actress, fell in love with Búzios and made it her second home. Her statue is now a main attraction, and the boardwalk was named Orla Bardot in her honour.

The reason Búzios is so appealing to me is not only because of its heavenly beaches but because of its ability to keep nature intact. The paths to the shore remain so unmarked by modernity that you feel as though you've strayed back a century in time with the dusty roads and improvised trails.

With it comes another aspect that I love about Búzios: the lack of foreign influence in its food. In Búzios you can truly eat like a fisherman. No matter what beach you stay in, *comida típica Buziana* (typical food from Búzios) is served. Grilled fish, salads, sandwiches and lots of different juices are just a few of the delicious foods of Búzios.

They are the inspiration for recipes to follow like Farfalle with Salmon and Caipirinha Sauce, inspired by a fish market (page 146), and Seven Fruit Salad, inspired by Geribá beach (page 149), while others are inspired by the effervescent night life of Búzios like the *crepe dos reis* (from Chez Michou, page 145).

COZINHA TIPICA BUZIANA

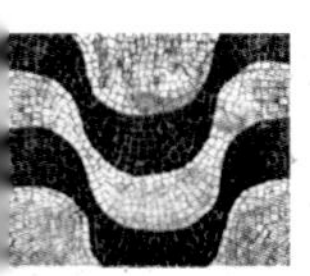

Suco de Abacaxi com Hortelã

PINEAPPLE AND MINT SMOOTHIE

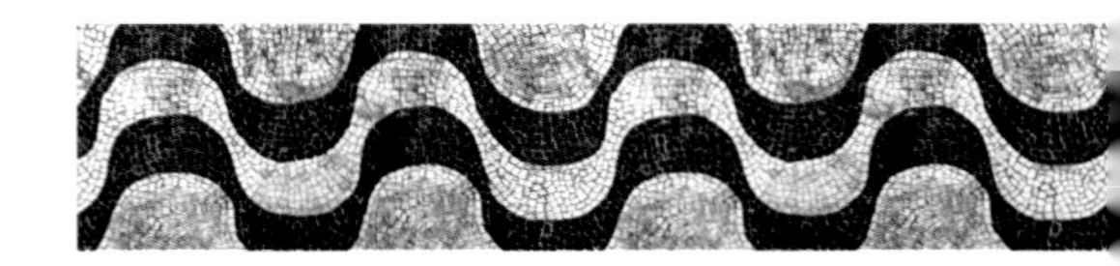

This simple smoothie is good for you, but that's not the only reason to give it a try. It is also a delicious little piece of Rio, where pineapples are as sweet as honey, that you can make at home in seconds for an instant pick-me-up. It doesn't require any exotic ingredients or techniques, and the combination of pineapple and mint packs this smoothie with a blast of brightness. Pick a fruit that feels heavy for its size, has a fresh fragrance and gives slightly when pressed at the base. The vendors at the market in Rio tap on the pineapples, searching for the sound of ripeness, like a full drum compared to a hollow one, and that's how I pick my pineapples too.

SERVES 1

325g cubed pineapple (about ½ pineapple)

8g mint leaves

1–2 tablespoons sugar, to taste

125ml water, plus extra if needed

Place the pineapple, mint leaves and sugar in a blender. Add the water and blend until smooth. Serve in a highball glass over ice.

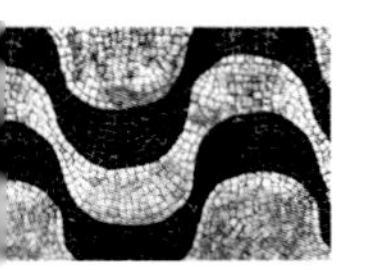

Crepe Chez Michouz
BRIE AND APRICOT CRÊPES

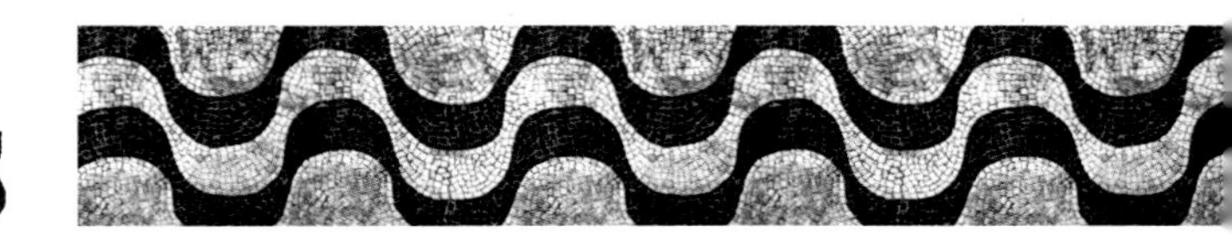

Chez Michou opened in 1983, when Búzios offered very little in terms of gastronomy, by two Argentineans and three Belgians who were looking to make Búzios their hometown. Located on the trendy Rua das Pedras, it's easier to get a table at Chez Michou during the day, but if you want to understand what Búzios is all about, go at night and you'll see one of the most buzzed-about places on earth, especially during Christmas and New Year. Sometimes the crowd is so big you can't even get close to the restaurant. But that's the charm of Rua das Pedras: it's a place to see and be seen.

When I was a young adult still living in Rio, we would go to Chez Michou to try to find the men of our dreams, but instead I found the crêpes of my dreams. Their crêpes come in a variety of flavours, both savoury and sweet. One of my favourites is *crepe dos reis* (king's crêpe) with the classic combination of Brie and jam. It's light and refreshing yet satisfying and indulgent.

MAKES 10

2 medium eggs

250ml full-fat milk

⅛ teaspoon salt

1½ tablespoons sugar

15g unsalted butter, melted, plus extra for cooking

80g plain flour

160g apricot jam

225g Brie cheese, at room temperature, cut into 6mm-thick slices, then cut into 2.5cm pieces

Icing sugar, for dusting

Place the eggs, milk, salt and sugar in a food processor or blender and process until smooth. Add the melted butter and process until combined. Add the flour and process until just incorporated. The flour should be completely blended, but don't overprocess.

Pour the batter into a large measuring jug or a large plastic container, cover and chill for at least 1 hour. The batter will thicken as it chills, but it should pour easily (if it's too thick, add a few drops of milk).

Whisk the batter if any foam has formed on top. Heat a small non-stick frying pan over a medium heat. Drop a pea-sized piece of butter into the pan and swirl it around. Working fast, pour in 2–3 tablespoons of batter, just to thinly coat the pan base. Cook for about 2 minutes until the underside is golden (take a peek using an angled palette knife). Flip it over and cook the other side for about 1 minute. (The second side never looks as handsome as the first side, coming out with dark spots.)

Transfer to a chopping board (nice side facing down) and spread a thin layer of apricot jam on top. Add 2 or 3 pieces of Brie and fold the crêpe in half. (If you prefer, fold the crêpe in quarters.) Repeat with the remaining batter and crêpes. (You can prepare the crêpes ahead of time and keep them stacked and wrapped in the fridge; to reheat, wrap the stack in foil and bake in a preheated 180°C/Gas Mark 4 oven for 5 minutes.) Dust with icing sugar and serve warm.

RESTAURANT: Chez Michou Crêperie, Av. José Bento Ribeiro Dantas, 90 Armação dos Búzios - Búzios, chezmichou.com.br

COOKING TIPS: As with any crêpe, the batter is quite simple to make and can be prepared up to 2 days ahead of time, kept in the fridge. I don't mind the rind on the Brie, but if you don't like it, go ahead and remove it.

Farfalle com Salmon ao Molho de Caipirinha

FARFALLE WITH SALMON AND CAIPIRINHA SAUCE

Búzios is known for its famous beaches, but also for its *pescadores*, or fishermen, true heroes who provide many fish markets in Rio with fresh fish. A trip to the fish market in Búzios makes my head spin. At the crack of dawn the market displays rows and rows of white plastic bins filled with ice and about 22kg worth of whole fish in each – red snapper, tuna, salmon, lobsters, octopus and many more – that were unloaded from boats just a few hours earlier. They also sell directly to the customer, so the last time I was there, before going back to Rio I bought a piece of salmon (and lots of ice for the three-hour car drive) and used it to create this easy and elegant dish rooted in carioca groove. Here is how it works. You roast the salmon and flake it. Make a sauce based on shallots, add stock (it can be fish, chicken or pasta water) and then, *ta-da*, you throw in the flavours of a caipirinha: cachaça, lime zest and lime juice, so that the pasta and fish get drunk in caipirinha flavours, just like a carioca.

SERVES 4

340g skin-on salmon fillet

Sea salt and freshly ground black pepper

300g dried farfalle pasta

2 tablespoons extra virgin olive oil, plus extra for oiling

1 large shallot, finely chopped

500ml chicken stock

250ml double cream

80ml cachaça

Finely grated zest of 1 lime

2 tablespoons fresh lime juice

10g fresh coriander, chopped

Preheat the oven to 180°C/Gas Mark 4.

Season the salmon with salt and pepper on both sides, place on an oiled baking sheet and roast for 6–8 minutes until almost cooked through. Remove from the oven and leave to cool slightly, then flake the fish into big chunks. Keep covered.

Bring a large saucepan of water to the boil over a high heat and add a good pinch of salt. Add the pasta and cook according to the packet instructions until al dente. Drain, reserving some of the cooking water, and transfer the pasta to a bowl.

Meanwhile, heat the olive oil in a large frying pan over a medium heat. Add the shallot and cook, stirring occasionally, for about 4 minutes until softened but not browned. Add the chicken stock, bring to the boil and cook for about 3 minutes until it just starts to reduce. Add the cream, reduce the heat to low and cook for about 5 minutes until it starts to thicken. Season lightly with salt and pepper.

Remove from the heat and stir in the cachaça and lime zest and juice. Add the pasta and salmon and heat over a low heat, tossing with tongs, until the fish is just heated through. Add the coriander and toss. Taste and adjust the seasonings if needed. If the dish needs a little more liquid, add some of the reserved pasta water.

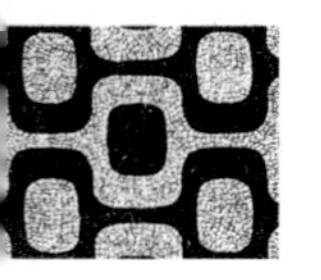

Sanduiche de Atum

TUNA SANDWICH

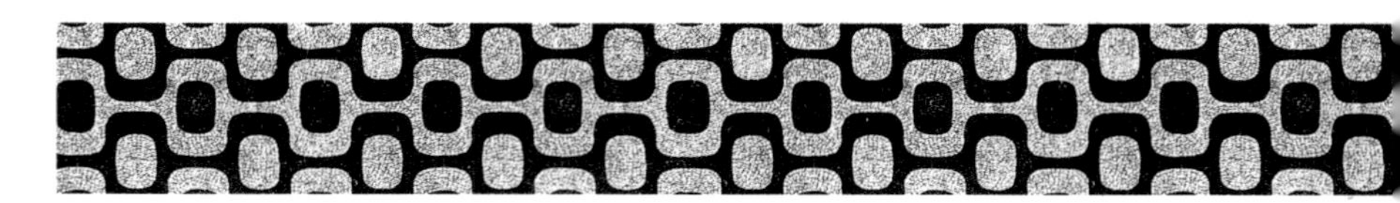

Growing up in Rio, there were three classic cold sandwiches a carioca would eat for lunch: egg salad sandwich, chicken salad sandwich (see page 135) and tuna salad sandwich. I was almost 25 before I realised that this trio of sandwiches existed in other countries. This recipe is inspired by a sandwich I ate at Sukão in Búzios that uses tomatoes (I use cherry tomatoes), lettuce (I substituted rocket) and wholemeal bread (but feel free to use any type).

MAKES 4

285g canned tuna, preferably in olive oil, drained and flaked

1 tablespoon finely chopped shallots

½ celery stick, finely diced

3 tablespoons coarsely chopped black olives

65g mayonnaise

Few drops of fresh lime juice

2 tablespoons chopped fresh dill

Sea salt and freshly ground black pepper

8 slices wholemeal bread

115g (about 12) cherry tomatoes, quartered

85g rocket

RESTAURANT: Sukâo Bar,
Praca Eugenio Honold,
Barrio Ossos - Buzios

Combine the tuna, shallots, celery, olives, mayonnaise, lime juice and dill in a large bowl. Season with salt and pepper and mix well. Cover and refrigerate for at least 1 hour for the flavours to develop.

Lightly toast the bread.

Fold the tomatoes into the tuna mixture, then divide the mixture between the bread slices, top with the rocket and sandwich together.

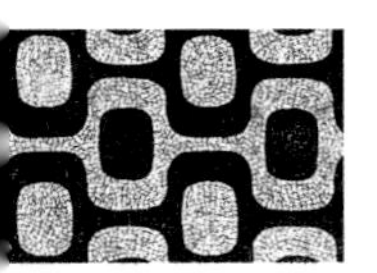

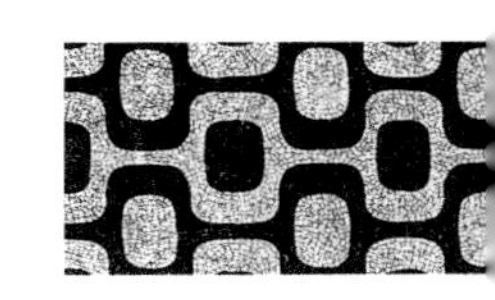

Salada de Frutas

SEVEN FRUIT SALAD WITH COCONUT FLAKES AND FRESH MINT

Salada de frutas is another staple of carioca cuisine and is standard beach food. This recipe is inspired by a version I tried in Búzios and can be made with a variety of fruits. Use this recipe as a guideline; any melon, citrus or stone fruit can be added. I like to add honey because it dissolves nicely into the orange juice, but an equal amount of sugar will work as well. Once the orange juice is mixed and the salad sits, the fruit starts losing its bright colour and shape, so pour the juice just before serving. This fruit salad is served for dessert; if you want to jazz it up, finish it with a dollop of whipped cream or a scoop of vanilla ice cream.

SERVES 4–6

60g dried flaked coconut

175ml fresh orange juice

2 tablespoons runny honey

195g diced pineapple (about ¼ pineapple)

185g diced mang (about 1 mango)

125g raspberries

135g hulled strawberries (about 6), quartered

175g seedless red grapes, halved

185g diced ripe papaya (about 1)

170g diced banana (about 2)

1 teaspoon finely grated lime zest

2 tablespoons chopped fresh mint

Preheat the oven to 150°C/Gas Mark 2.

Spread the coconut out on a small baking sheet and toast in the oven for about 4 minutes, rotating the sheet once, until it is very lightly browned. Transfer to a bowl and set aside.

Whisk the orange juice and honey together in a small bowl.

Combine all the fruit in a large bowl and gently mix with a spatula. Pour in the orange juice-honey mixture and add the lime zest and mint. Fold carefully to coat the fruit.

Pour into serving bowls, decorate with the toasted coconut and serve the fruit salads immediately.

10

BARCO≈GANDHY≈
ALUGA-SE≈PASSEIO≈
E PESCA
LOTAÇÃO≈ 14+1
TEL (CEL) 88112348
CAPITANIA TEL 33711583

PARATY

PARATY: A COASTAL TOWN

Paraty is located on the coast between Rio de Janeiro and São Paulo; it was founded in 1667. The soil around the region is perfect for sugar cane plantations, and since the old days the region has been cluttered with mills producing cachaça. During the seventeeth and eighteenth centuries, a triangular path linking Rio de Janeiro to Minas Gerais and São Paulo known as *Caminho do Ouro* (the gold path) brought even more prosperity to Paraty, as its harbours strategically served as a place to ship gold to Portugal.

The histories of cachaça and Paraty are intertwined on cultural, economic and social levels. The city consists of a harbour crowded with tourist boats, four churches and the historic centre, in which you'll find charming boutiques selling crafts and cachaça from the mills of the region, which are more active now than ever. As a caipirinha devotee, I got lost in a store called Armazém da Cachaça, which sells hundreds of cachaças of every taste: sweet, salty, spicy, blended, aged in carvalho wood and jequitibá. Just a few blocks away, another store, Espaço da Cachaça, offered the same kind of experience. This cachaça bonanza inspired the delicious caipi-coco cake, on page 158.

Other recipes in this chapter are inspired by a visit to a typical Paraty restaurant called Banana da Terra, where you'll find plenty of fish dishes but it was their *bolinha de queijo* (page 155) that made me swoon, and the fish boats of Paraty, where I bought prawns for the roasted garlic-ginger recipe on page 157.

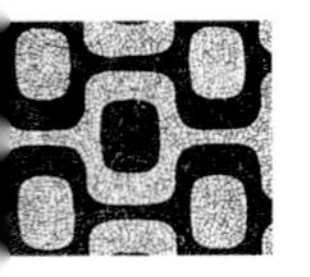

Batida de Côco
COCONUT COCKTAIL

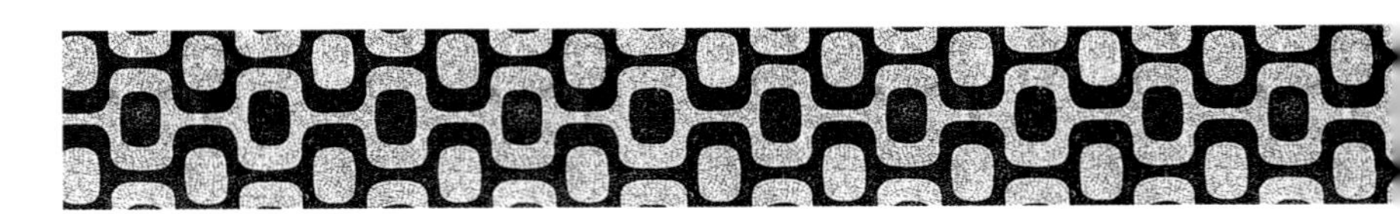

Batida de côco is a classic cocktail served at all the bars in Rio, and this version is inspired by the many *cachaçarias* around Paraty. A vendor at the store Armazém da Cachaça told me that he likes to mix vodka and cachaça, which is what I do here. The cocktail is lighter using this combination, though you can use only cachaça if you prefer. I generally like my cocktails on the lighter side, but you can feel free to use a stronger dose of either or both of the spirits than what I suggest here.

SERVES 6

200ml coconut milk

397g can sweetened condensed milk

250ml vodka

60ml cachaça

40g unsweetened desiccated coconut

Combine all the ingredients in a blender and blend until smooth. Pour into ice-filled glasses and serve.

Bolinha de Queijo

CHEESE FRITTERS

RESTAURANT: Bannana Da Terra
Rua Dr Samuel Costa 198 - Paraty
restaurantebananadaterra.com.br

This recipe is based on a snack that is served at Banana Da Terra, a restaurant in Paraty. These crisp little nuggets of cheese dough provide a wonderful crunch and then melt in your mouth. You can't eat just one. *Bolinha de queijo* is a classic botequim food from the 1980s that disappeared from restaurant menus for a while but is increasingly, and with good reason, showing up all over Rio again. Ana Bueno, the chef behind this lovely restaurant, likes to serve these with a dollop of plantain purée stuffed inside, but I skipped that step in the interest of keeping things simple.

MAKES ABOUT 50

115g unsalted butter

40ml extra virgin olive oil

40g shallot, very finely chopped

Sea salt and freshly ground black pepper

95g cornflour

500ml full-fat milk

200g plain flour

Pinch of cayenne pepper

Freshly grated nutmeg

50g Parmesan cheese, finely grated

225g provolone cheese, cut into 2cm cubes

625ml vegetable oil, for frying

1 medium egg, lightly beaten

65g dried breadcrumbs

Melt the butter in the olive oil in a medium saucepan over a low heat. Add the shallot and cook for about 3 minutes until softened. Season lightly with salt and pepper.

Whisk the cornflour with the milk in a small bowl. Pour the mixture into the pan with the shallots and cook, stirring constantly with a wooden spoon, for 2–3 minutes until it thickens.

Add the flour all at once, reduce the heat to low and continue to cook; the dough will start coming together and a thin crust will form on the base of the pan. Season with salt, pepper, the cayenne and nutmeg. Continue cooking, mashing the dough with a wooden spoon, for 8–10 minutes until it forms a smooth, glossy paste. Transfer to a bowl and leave to cool to room temperature.

Add the Parmesan and mix with a wooden spoon. Using a tablespoon, scoop little mounds of dough, stuff each with a cube of provolone cheese and close the balls, pinching with your fingers and rolling in your hands to make 2.5cm balls.

Pour the vegetable oil into a heavy-based saucepan and heat to 180°C, as measured by a deep-fat thermometer. If you don't have a thermometer, pour a drip of batter into the oil; when you hear a sizzling sound and see the batter turning golden brown, the oil is ready. Preheat the oven to 110°C/Gas Mark ¼.

While the oil is heating, place the egg in a shallow bowl and the breadcrumbs in another. Pass each fritter through the eggs, then the breadcrumbs, shaking off the excess.

Add the *bolinhas* to the oil in batches, only adding as many as will fit without touching each other. Fry, turning them occasionally so that they brown evenly on all sides, for about 3 minutes per batch. Transfer to a baking sheet covered with kitchen paper. Keep the finished batches in the warm oven on a baking sheet until all are fried.

Camarão Assado aos Sabores do Brazil

ROASTED GARLIC-GINGER PRAWNS WITH COCONUT AND FRESH HERB CRUMBS

On a recent trip to Paraty, I came across a fishing boat with prawns for sale. I bought a few pounds and asked the fisherman for an idea on how to cook my crustaceans. He said, *'Oh Senhora, eu uso os nossos temperos, ponho no forno, e fica uma delícia'* ('Oh lady, I use Brazilian seasonings and it comes out delicious'). At first I was unhappy with his vague answer, but then the words *nosso temperos* kept circling in my mind. After all, we have tons of spices. I usually stick to prawn recipes that pair them with another main ingredient, such as pasta with prawns, rice with prawns and *shrimp moqueca*, but this time I wanted to cook the prawns by themselves, and this dish, bright and boldly flavoured with the Brazilian seasonings, is now my favourite solo prawn recipe.

SERVES 4

4 tablespoons *dendê* (palm) oil, plus extra for oiling (you can substitute olive oil)

6 garlic cloves, very finely chopped

1 tablespoon grated fresh ginger

1 spring onion, white and green parts, finely chopped

1 tablespoon chopped fresh parsley

1 tablespoon chopped fresh coriander

½ teaspoon very finely chopped jalapeño pepper

Sea salt

900g raw large king prawns, peeled and deveined,

HERB CRUMB

4 tablespoons *dendê* (palm) oil

95g toasted manioc flour (*farinha de mandioca fina; see page 41*) or dried breadcrumbs

25g unsweetened desiccated coconut

2 tablespoons chopped fresh parsley

2 tablespoons chopped fresh cilantro

125ml dry white wine

Preheat the oven to 190°C/Gas Mark 5.

In a large bowl, combine the *dendê* oil with the garlic, ginger, spring onion, parsley, coriander, jalapeño and salt to taste. Add the prawns and toss everything together. Cover and refrigerate for 10 minutes.

Make the herb crumb: In a small bowl, combine the *dendê* oil with the manioc flour, coconut, parsley, coriander and salt to taste.

Lightly oil a 23cm x 33cm baking dish. Lay each prawn in the dish with the back side flat like a book and the tail end standing straight up. Pour in the wine, then sprinkle the crumb mixture loosely over the prawns. Place the dish in the oven and roast for 12–15 minutes until the prawns turn pink. Serve immediately.

Bolo de Caipirinha com Côco

CAIPIRINHA COCONUT CAKE

On a visit to Paraty where I sampled a variety of different cachaças, I started to think of the desserts I could make using the flavours of caipirinha. Dancing in my head were visions of tender caipirinha cake, exploding with Brazilian flavours. Lime, cachaça, butter, eggs and coconut milk were no-brainers. I turned to Rose Levy Beranbaum for a little tech support, and was rewarded with a nutty, light, gently flavoured caipirinha cake. When it was all gone I immediately wanted to make it again and invited some friends over for dinner as an excuse. This time coconut milk was sold out at the supermarket and only cream of coconut was available. I made the cake with the cream of coconut, sneaking a spoonful for quality control purposes. The flavour was markedly different from the previous batch, more creamy, perhaps because of the extra fat from the coconut cream.

Then I decided my cake needed to get drunk, so I made a caipirinha syrup, and to round out my creation I came up with a caipirinha whipped cream. The cake was so much fun to make and so easy to eat, we nearly devoured it all in one sitting. I nicknamed it Caipi-Coco Cake, and it is now a typical Saturday night dessert in my house – along with caipirinhas, of course.

SERVES 8–10

190g coconut cream

3 medium (90g) egg whites

2 tablespoons cachaça

1 teaspoon lemon extract

90g sugar

35g unsweetened desiccated coconut

Finely grated zest of 1 lime

200g cake flour, plus extra for dusting

2¼ teaspoons baking powder

½ teaspoon salt

150g unsalted butter, plus extra for greasing

40g dried flaked coconut, for topping

Preheat the oven to 180°C/Gas Mark 4. Grease a 23cm round, 5cm deep cake pan and line the base with baking parchment, then coat the baking parchment with butter and dust with flour, tapping out the excess.

Combine the coconut cream, egg whites, cachaça and lemon extract in a medium bowl and whisk until well combined.

Combine the sugar, desiccated coconut and lime zest in a food processor and process for about 1 minute until the oils from the coconut and lime zest infuse the sugar.

Sift the flour, baking powder and salt into a large bowl.

Cream the butter with the sugar–coconut–lime zest mixture in the bowl of an electric mixer fitted with the paddle attachment at medium speed for about 3 minutes until light and creamy, stopping and scraping the sides of the bowl occasionally.

Reduce the speed to low and add half of the cream of coconut mixture – the batter will curdle, and that's okay, as it will come together when you add the remaining ingredients. Continue beating slowly.

Add half of the dry ingredients, alternating with the remaining coconut cream mixture (begin with the liquid and end with the dry ingredients), and beat until just combined, scraping the sides of the bowl. Scrape the batter into the prepared pan and smooth the surface with an angled palette knife.

Bake for 30–40 minutes until golden brown, the cake starts to shrink from the sidesof the tin and a skewer inserted in the centre the comes out clean.

CAIPIRINHA SYRUP

120g sugar

60ml fresh lime juice

2 tablespoons cachaça

CAIPI-COCO WHIPPED CREAM

350g double cream

1–2 tablespoons icing sugar, sifted

1 teaspoon cachaça

Finely grated zest of 1 lime

Meanwhile, make the caipirinha syrup. Combine the sugar and lime juice in a small saucepan and gently warm over a low heat, whisking constantly, for about 4 minutes until the sugar is dissolved. Don't let it boil. Transfer to a bowl and add the cachaça.

Transfer the cake tin to a wire rack and reduce the oven temperature to 150°C/Gas Mark 2. Immediately poke the cake several times with a thin skewer and brush the cake with the syrup (it's important to soak the cake while still hot). Leave the cake to cool in the tin for at least 30 minutes, then invert onto a serving plate.

While the cake is cooling, spread the flaked coconut onto a small baking sheet and toast in the oven for 4–6 minutes until lightly browned.

Make the caipi-coco whipped cream. Beat the cream with the icing sugar in the bowl of an electric mixer fitted with the whisk attachment until soft peaks form. Turn off the mixer, add the cachaça and lime zest and whisk them in by hand. Spread the cream on top of the cake and sprinkle evenly with the toasted coconut. Serve immediately.

11

REGIAO SERRANA

A TRIBUTE TO TERESÓPOLIS IN REGIANO SERRANA

A few miles and a world away north of Rio lies a city called Teresópolis. Part of the mountain region that serves as the weekend getaway for many cariocas, Teresópolis is slightly shadowed by its sister cities Petrópolis and Itaipava. The trio has much in common in terms of offering a weekend of fun and retreat to cariocas, and many people transit from one city to another during the weekend.

Petrópolis, for instance, has a lovely museum, interesting local boutiques and nice restaurants. Teresópolis, although with fewer spotlights, was a larger part of my childhood. It's a city where nature still calls the shots. There isn't much to do or see, but there is a lot to eat.

Right from the city's entrance, you can hear the sound of running water. It's Fonte Judite, a fountain with water so clean that people bring gallon jugs to fill them up and take with them. Over the mountains we see the tallest peak, called Dedo de Deus ('Finger of God'), the portal of the city. Gargantuan pointy evergreens are everywhere, giving the tree line a jagged edge, like a serrated knife.

The fact that this city offers a colder climate brings a whole different gastronomic culture over the mountains. While in Rio salads, juices and light meals have an all-year-long appeal, in Teresópolis the cold climate gives one an opportunity to binge on comfort foods, chocolate desserts and hot drinks like the Brazilian mallomars (page 176) from Maria Torta and the Brazilian 'tiramisu' (page 172) that I include here. The *feirinha*, or outdoor market, provides a natural theatre for these feasts, where local foodies and artisans showcase their talents.

The city has a unique spirit, one that beckons to a progressive and outdoorsy group. People share a fondness for bikes, beards, tattoos, flannels and all-weather pullovers that lie far outside the norm of Rio.

Perhaps it's because I grew up coming to this city, or perhaps it's because the city hasn't changed much since then, but I still feel the wind rippling and wet air from my childhood in Teresópolis.

Caldo de Piranha

PIRANHA SOUP

RESTAURANT: Caldo da Piranha, R. Jose Elias Zaquem, 350 - Teresopolis

It's hard to imagine a restaurant in Teresópolis serving food from the midwest of Brazil. But in Caldo da Piranha, Mr Ernani Antonio de Oliveira's traditional restaurant established in 1994, this soup is a speciality. Though Mr Oliveira does not claim the creation of this recipe, his restaurant's popularity was built upon it. Twenty-five years ago he caught and cooked the dangerous piranha fish for the first time on a trip to Pantanal. He followed a well-known recipe, but as time went by, he perfected his own version, found a supplier in Vitória, Espírito Santo, and sold the dish in his son's snack bar. The success was instant, and his son transformed his bar into a restaurant specialising in his father's signature dish.

When I tasted the famous soup, I quickly understood how deeply pleasing are the prized flavours of the piranha; with a rich creaminess that comes without the addition of cream, this hearty and earthy soup can be served as a starter or as a main course.

SERVES 4

1 whole sea bass, gutted, scaled, head and tail removed (about 680g)

Sea salt and freshly ground black pepper

4 tablespoons olive oil

3 garlic cloves, chopped

1 small onion, chopped

3 spring onions, white and green parts, finely chopped

3 plum tomatoes, peeled, deseeded and chopped

3 tablespoons plain flour

1 tablespoon chopped fresh parsley

1 tablespoon chopped fresh coriander

Cut the fish into large chunks and season with salt and pepper.

Heat 2 tablespoons of the olive oil in a large flameproof casserole dish over a medium heat. Add the fish and cook, turning occasionally, for about 4 minutes until it starts to turn opaque. Depending on the fish, the skin might stick to the base of the pan, and that's okay; you can scrape it later. Add enough water to cover the fish, about 700ml, cover the pan and bring to the boil. Reduce the heat to low and simmer gently for about 5 minutes until the fish is cooked through, skimming off any foam that bubbles to the surface.

Using a slotted spoon, transfer the fish to a bowl. When cool enough to handle, finely shred the fish, discarding the skin and bones, and cover with foil. Strain the liquid and reserve it in a separate bowl.

In the same pan, heat the remaining 2 tablespoons olive oil over a low heat, add the garlic and cook for about 2 minutes until lightly browned. Add the onion and spring onions and cook, stirring frequently, for about 3 minutes until they are softened. Add the tomatoes and cook for 2–3 minutes until they just start to release their liquid. Season lightly with salt and pepper. Transfer to a food processor (a mini food processor if you have one) and process for about 1 minute until smooth. Scrape back into the same pan.

Add the flour and cook for 1–2 minutes over a medium heat. Pour in the reserved liquid from the fish, whisking well, and simmer the soup for about 10 minutes until it thickens, adding a little more water if it gets too thick. Add the shredded fish and season with salt and pepper.

To serve, ladle the soup into individual soup bowls and garnish with the parsley and coriander. (The soup can be kept covered in the fridge for up to 2 days. It reheats very well.)

INGREDIENT NOTE: You can make this soup using fish fillet instead of whole fish. In this case, add 700ml fish, prawn or chicken stock, as you won't be making your own fish stock. Since chances are slim that we'll find piranha outside Brazil, I used sea bass here; red snapper and pompano can also work.

Porco na Cerveja

PORK IN BEER

RESTAURANT: Vila St. Gallen
Rua Augusto do Amaral Peixoto, 166 - Teresopolis

Teresópolis, a mountain city one hour north of Rio, has a new attraction: Vila St Gallen, an artisanal brewery and restaurant specialising in German beer and food. In Rio beer has always been associated with a toast – a reward for a finished project, the gorgeous beaches of Rio or simply the celebration of life. There is plenty to celebrate with a beer in a glass. But after a visit to Vila St Gallen, I began to appreciate the potential of using beer as an ingredient.

Beer works nicely with meat, so, inspired by Vila, I came up with this pork in beer stew. I developed this recipe using the beer from Vila St. Galen, but you can use any full-bodied beer in this recipe. I wanted to get my pork completely drunk, so I marinated it overnight to infuse the meat with that sweet and bitter beer taste. Then I lightly browned the pork and braised it in the oven with aromatic vegetables and new potatoes as an accompaniment.

SERVES 4–6

900g boneless pork shoulder, excess fat removed, cut into 2.5cm chunks

1 large onion, quartered

2 celery sticks, cut into large chunks

2 medium carrots, cut into large chunks

3 garlic cloves, lightly crushed

3 fresh bay leaves

2 x 330ml bottles of beer, such as Stella Artois

Sea salt and freshly ground black pepper

3 tablespoons extra virgin olive oil, plus extra if needed

5 plum tomatoes, peeled, deseeded and roughly chopped

1 litre chicken stock

680g small new potatoes, peeled and quartered

3 tablespoons chopped fresh parsley

Place the pork, onion, celery, carrots, garlic and bay leaves in a large zip-seal freezer bag. Pour in the beer, distribute well in the bag and seal it, making sure all the air is out. Leave to marinate in the fridge for at least 4 hours, or preferably overnight.

Preheat the oven to 180°C/Gas Mark 4.

Separate the pork from the vegetables and strain the liquid. Reserve all. Place the pork on a baking sheet lined with kitchen paper and air-dry for 5 minutes. Pat dry to remove any excess moisture. Season with salt and pepper.

Pour the beer into a small saucepan and bring to the boil over a medium heat. Foam will rise to the surface; skim and remove it, then cook for 4–5 minutes until 120–180ml is left. Strain into a measuring jug.

Heat the olive oil in a large, deep frying pan or flameproof casserole dish over a high heat and, working in batches if necessary, sear the pork for about 4 minutes until lightly browned all over. Transfer to a bowl and cover with foil to keep moist.

Reduce the heat to low and add the vegetables to the pan, adding more oil if necessary. Season lightly with salt and pepper and cook, stirring with a wooden spoon and scraping the browned bits from the base of the pan, for about 5 minutes until the vegetables are softened and translucent.

Add the tomatoes and cook about 2 minutes until softened. Season lightly with salt and pepper. Add the beer and chicken stock and bring to the boil over a high heat.

Add the pork and any juices accumulated in the bowl. Cover the pan, place in the oven and braise for 1 hour. Discard the large pieces of carrot and celery (I leave the onions), add the potatoes, cover and continue to braise for 30–35 minutes until the pork is very tender and the potatoes are just tender. Garnish with the parsley and serve.

Panquecas de Espinafre

SPINACH CRÊPES WITH FRESH TOMATO SAUCE

Ivani de Souza Ferreira is a woman who makes a living from the art of cooking. She grew up around food and learned to cook by watching other people, so when I asked if she could share a recipe for this book, I was expecting she would have at least a notebook with recipes archived. But everything she cooks comes straight from the bank of knowledge she has inside her head; she never follows a recipe. The best part about cooking with her is tapping into that knowledge there in the kitchen. More about that in the next recipe. This one that Ivani shared is healthy, light, nutritious and super delicious! Take this recipe as a guideline; from here you can add different mushrooms or Gorgonzola, or your choice of additional ingredients to the spinach.

SERVES 4–6 OR MAKES 8–10 CRÊPES

80g plain flour

125ml full-fat milk

60ml lukewarm water

30g unsalted butter, melted and cooled

2 medium eggs, lightly beaten

½ teaspoon sea salt

Olive oil, for cooking the crêpes

SPINACH FILLING

2 tablespoons salt, plus extra for seasoning

280g fresh spinach

15g unsalted butter

2 garlic cloves, very finely chopped

1 small shallot, very finely chopped

180ml chicken stock

2 tablespoons plain flour

Freshly ground black pepper

Freshly grated nutmeg

Combine the flour, milk, water, butter, eggs and salt in a blender and blend for 1–2 minutes until you have a very smooth batter. Transfer to a bowl, cover and refrigerate for at least 30 minutes.

Meanwhile, make the spinach filling. Bring 1 litre water to the boil in a large saucepan and add the salt. Trim any thick stems from the spinach. Add the spinach to the boiling water and cook for about 1 minute until just softened. Drain the spinach into a colander and press on it to remove the excess liquid. Leave the spinach to drain for 5 minutes, then roughly chop it.

Melt the butter in a medium saucepan. Add the garlic and cook for about 1 minute until just golden. Add the shallot and cook for 1 minute until softened. Stir in the spinach, then remove the pan from the heat.

Heat the chicken stock in a small saucepan over a low heat. Place the flour in a small bowl, add a few tablespoons of the stock and whisk well. Pour the mixture back into the stock pan and cook, whisking constantly, for about 3 minutes until it starts to thicken. Season with salt, pepper and nutmeg. Mix the spinach into the chicken stock. Taste again, adjust the seasonings if necessary and remove from the heat.

Make the tomato sauce. Melt the butter in a medium saucepan over a low heat, add the garlic and cook for about 1 minute until just golden. Add the onion and cook for about 5 minutes until softened. Add the tomatoes and cook, stirring frequently, for a further 2 minutes until they begin to soften. Add the water, increase the heat to medium and bring to the boil, then add the tomato sauce. Season with salt and pepper. Cook for 10–15 minutes until nice and tasty.

Preheat the oven to 180°C/Gas Mark 4. Grease a 23cm x 33cm baking dish with butter.

Heat a small non-stick frying pan over a low heat. Add about 1 teaspoon olive oil and swirl the pan around to coat the bottom. Pour in 2–3 tablespoons of the batter and immediately swirl the pan to spread the batter into a thin, even round. Cook for about 2 minutes until the underside turns gorgeously golden brown (take a peek), then, using an angled palette knife, flip and cook the other side for about 2 minutes

TOMATO SAUCE

15g butter, plus extra for greasing

2 garlic cloves, very finely chopped

½ onion, chopped

2 plum tomatoes, peeled, deseeded and diced

125ml water

2 x 227g cans tomato sauce

Sea salt and freshly ground black pepper

50g Parmesan cheese, freshly grated

until you see black spots (the second side is never as pretty as the first). Transfer to a baking sheet and repeat with the remaining batter.

Fill each crêpe with 2–3 tablespoons of the spinach, then roll it tightly. Arrange the crêpes in the prepared baking dish and spoon some tomato sauce on top. (You might not use all of the tomato sauce.) Sprinkle the Parmesan on top and bake for about 12 minutes until the cheese is melted and the sauce is bubbling. Serve immediately.

COOKING TIP: If you want to add a bit more flavour to the topping, try substituting Gruyère for the Parmesan cheese. You can also use frozen spinach; if you do so, simply thaw it rather than blanch it. You can prepare the dish ahead of time and keep it covered in the fridge for up to 2 days.

Empadão de Palmito da Ivani

IVANI'S HEARTS OF PALM TART

In cooking school, I learned how to make chicken stock and veal stock and all the other foundational stocks. In the professional world, stock cubes are looked at with disdain. When I watched Ivani de Souza Ferreira prepare this wonderful tart, my world turned upside down when I saw her using a stock in it. At first I just couldn't grasp what she was doing. I kept asking her, 'Where is the water? Aren't you going to dissolve it in water?' She just looked at me, smiled and continued cooking. From that day on, the stock cube has become one of my favourite seasonings.

SERVES 6–8

DOUGH

500g all-purpose flour, plus extra for dusting

1 teaspoon salt

255g unsalted butter, chilled and cubed

3 medium egg yolks

4 tablespoons ice-cold water

HEARTS OF PALM FILLING

250ml full-fat milk

3 tablespoons plain flour

Sea salt and freshly ground black pepper

30g unsalted butter

4 garlic cloves, very finely chopped

1 onion, chopped

3 plum tomatoes peeled, deseeded and diced

250ml chicken stock cube (preferably Knorr)

750g hearts of palm, sliced into 6mm-thick rings, or about 4 x 400g cans, drained

2 tablespoons chopped green olives (optional)

Make the dough. Combine the flour and salt in the bowl of a food processor. Add the butter and pulse until it looks like coarse breadcrumbs. Add the egg yolks and water and continue to pulse until the dough just starts to come together (depending on the humidity, you might need a few drops more of water). Place the dough on a floured surface and gather it into a ball, then divide it in half and shape it into 2 flat discs. Wrap in clingfilm and refrigerate for at least 30 minutes (this can be done up to 2 days ahead).

Next, make the filling. Warm the milk in a small saucepan over a low heat. Place the flour in a small bowl, add 2–3 tablespoons of the milk and whisk well to dissolve. Pour back into the saucepan and cook over a low heat, whisking constantly, for about 3 minutes until thickened. Season with salt and pepper. Remove from the heat, cover and set aside. Melt the butter in a medium saucepan over a low heat, add the garlic and cook for about 2 minutes until just starting to turn golden. Add the onion and cook for about 2 minutes until softened. Add the tomatoes and cook for about 3 minutes until everything blends. Crumble in the stock cube and mix well with a wooden spatula to dissolve it. Add the hearts of palm and fold everything together. Add the green olives, if using, and the parsley and season lightly with salt and pepper.

Pour the thickened milk into the hearts of palm mixture and fold it in. Taste again and adjust the seasoning if needed. Spread the mixture onto a baking tray and refrigerate for at least 30 minutes (this can be prepared up to 2 days ahead of time).

Remove the dough from the fridge at least 20 minutes before rolling it so that it becomes malleable. Roll out the first piece of dough on a lightly floured surface into a round about 3mm thick, lifting the dough often and making sure that the work surface and the dough are amply floured at all times. Roll the dough up and around your rolling pin, then unroll it into a 23cm springform cake tin, fitting the dough into the bottom and up the sides of the tin. If the dough cracks or splits as you work, don't worry – you can patch the cracks with scraps using a wet finger to 'glue' them in place.

Spoon the filling evenly across the dough. Using a pastry brush dipped in water, lightly moisten the exposed edges of the pastry case.

20g fresh parsley, chopped

1 medium egg, beaten, for egg wash

Roll the remaining dough into a round and transfer to the top of the tin, pressing against the pastry case with your fingers, then trim the overhang from both the case and lid, making sure they are securely sealed together.

Cut an X in the centre to serve as a steam vent. Refrigerate for at least 20 minutes before baking.

Position a shelf at the centre of the oven and preheat the oven to 190°C/Gas Mark 5. Place the tart on a baking sheet and bake for about 30 minutes until the top is lightly browned. Remove the tart from the oven, brush the top with egg wash, return to the oven and bake for 10–15 minutes until the pastry is gorgeously browned. Transfer to a rack and leave to rest for 20 minutes before serving warm.

Strudel de Frango com Catupiry

SAVOURY STRUDELS WITH CHICKEN AND CATUPIRY CHEESE

When he arrived in Petrópolis, German immigrant Stefano Kern brought to Rio recipes from his native land. Together with other bakers, he opened Casa do Alemão. The first store opened on the highway from Rio to the mountain region, cariocas on their way out of the city regularly make this sacred stop at Casa do Alemão to eat their favourite snacks. This recipe is inspired by this German–carioca establishment. If you're wondering why you have to make two strudels instead of one, it's because the proportion of dough to filling just doesn't work with one large strudel. But this is not an easy recipe to simply halve, so I decided to make the strudel thinner and more elegant by splitting the dough – it's easier to handle, easier to bake and easier to present. You have the option of serving one strudel right away and keeping the other on a baking sheet covered in clingfilm in the fridge for up to 2 days before baking.

MAKES 2; SERVES 6–8

450g cooked chicken, shredded

2 tablespoons olive oil

1 onion, finely chopped

1 celery stick, finely chopped

3 garlic cloves, very finely chopped

2 plum tomatoes, peeled, deseeded and diced, or 5 tablespoons ready-made marinara pasta sauce

2 teaspoons dried oregano

Sea salt and freshly ground black pepper

Freshly grated nutmeg

2 tablespoons chopped fresh parsley

175ml chicken stock

15g butter

2 tablespoons plain flour, plus extra for dusting

Place the shredded chicken in a large bowl.

Heat the olive oil in a medium frying pan over a medium-low heat, add the onion and celery and cook for about 3 minutes until softened and translucent. Add the garlic and cook for another minute. Add the tomatoes and oregano and cook until the tomatoes are softened. Season with salt, pepper and nutmeg. Pour on top of the chicken, add the parsley and mix well.

Warm the chicken stock in a small saucepan. In a separate saucepan, melt the butter over a low heat. Immediately add the flour and cook until it starts to bubble lightly. Add the chicken stock and whisk vigorously, making sure there are no lumps. Season lightly with salt, pepper and nutmeg. Add to the chicken mixture and combine well. Taste and adjust the seasoning one more time. Refrigerate until cold. (You can make this filling up to 2 days ahead; keep covered in the fridge.)

Open the pastry onto a floured surface. Using a rolling pin, roll the dough into a 30cm x 46cm rectangle. Slide onto a baking sheet and refrigerate for 10 minutes.

Remove the dough from the fridge and cut vertically into 2 strips of 15cm x 46cm. Arrange each piece of dough on a sheet of baking parchment lightly dusted with flour for easy transfer to the baking sheet. Distribute the chicken filling equally and vertically along the 2 pieces of dough, leaving a 5cm border on all sides. Using a spoon, create a vertical path to receive the cheese. Place the cheese inside a piping bag without a piping tube (or a zip-seal freezer bag with the corner cut off) and squeeze a thick line of cheese right in the middle of the filling. Using a spatula, push some of the chicken on top to cover the cheese, keeping it from touching the dough.

12

HOME COOKING

FROM TANGIER TO RIO

When I speak English, most people recognise a foreign accent. Well, sure, I am from Brazil. When my father speaks Portuguese, the same happens. And when my aunt Sarita speaks Portuguese, they think she is a tourist!

Aunt Sarita is my father's oldest sister. She and my father were born in Tangier, Morocco, and emigrated to Brazil in 1960, when my aunt was 22, the same age I was when I moved to New York.

Recently I started to trace back my family's history. What brought them from Tangier to Rio? And where does my affinity for cooking come from? I know for sure it's not from my parents. Although they love to eat, my mother doesn't cook much beyond making fried eggs – something she does quite well – but only because that is one of her favourite foods to eat.

It all started with Aunt Sarita, or Tia Sarita as we say in Portuguese. She came to Brazil in 1958, while the rest of the family stayed in Tangier. Two years later, as the political situation worsened in Morocco, the rest of the family emigrated. My father was 11 years old when he came to Brazil. He still says the word Leblon – one of the most famous neighbourhoods in Rio, and where we live – with a French accent. The minute the words leave his lips, cariocas know he wasn't born in Brazil.

As I embarked on a quest to recover my family's recipes, I spent one of the most memorable afternoons of my life cooking with Tia Sarita and Neusa de Souza, an African Brazilian woman who helps my aunt. On a visit to her apartment in Rio de Janeiro, with the typical bright sun reflecting on their veranda, I asked my aunt to show me how to cook like a real Moroccan.

As I watched my aunt cook, I saw myself in her. The way she bends her body when she stirs the minced meat; the way her face hides a smile when the food turns out well; even the way her nose is as pointy as mine. I had no idea that by cooking with her I'd also find a part of myself.

For Tia Sarita, food remains the primary connection between her Moroccan roots and her new life in Brazil. After 50 years of living in Brazil, I can see in both my aunt and my father how Brazil has changed them – for the better. My father's devotion to fitness is a testament to his successful Brazilian acclimatisation, as is his love of cold beer accompanied by salt cod fritters and lots of loud friends. My aunt's relationship with Neusa de Souza, the woman who cooks with her and has absorbed the traditions of our family, is testament as well. All that joie de vivre that cariocas are known for has rubbed off on them, and today they are completely immersed in the culture of their adopted country.

There in the
You

TIA SARITA'S MOROCCAN MEATBALLS

It's the Moroccan spices that makes this recipe so interesting. My Aunt Sarita uses two kinds of paprika here: Hungarian, with a sweet taste and a vibrant red colour, and smoked Spanish (where peppers are smoked over an oak fire), with a richer taste and a darker red tone.

SERVES 4–6

MEATBALLS

450g beef mince

1 medium egg yolk

1 slice wholemeal bread, crusts removed, torn into small pieces

1 onion, very finely chopped

¼ teaspoon ground cinnamon

¼ teaspoon ground cumin

½ teaspoon Hungarian paprika

2 teaspoons smoked Spanish paprika

1 teaspoon ground coriander

1 tablespoon chopped fresh parsley

2 tablespoons olive oil

1½ teaspoons sea salt

Freshly ground black pepper

SAFFRON SAUCE

3 tablespoons olive oil

4 small onions, chopped

1 bay leaf

1½ teaspoons ground ginger

Pinch of saffron threads

1½ teaspoons ground cumin

½ teaspoon Hungarian paprika

½ teaspoon Spanish paprika

Pinch of ground turmeric

Sea salt and freshly ground black pepper

Juice of ½ lime

10g fresh parsley, chopped

10g fresh coriander, chopped

Place the beef, egg yolk, bread pieces, onion, parsley, olive oil and salt and a grind or two of pepper in a bowl and combine well with a rubber spatula or knead with your hands. Scoop a tiny portion and fry in a small frying pan to make sure the seasoning is just right. Refrigerate for at least 30 minutes, or preferably 2 hours.

Have a small bowl of water nearby, wet your hands and form the meat mixture into 1.25cm balls. Set aside on a plate until ready to cook.

Make the sauce. Warm the olive oil in a large deep saucepan over a medium-low heat. Add the onions and cook for about 6 minutes until softened and translucent. Add the bay leaf, ginger, saffron, cumin, Hungarian and Spanish paprika, turmeric and salt and pepper to taste and cook, stirring frequently with a wooden spoon, for 3–5 minutes until fragrant. Add 360ml hot water and bring to the boil.

Add the meatballs, reduce the heat to low, cover and poach them for 20 minutes, stirring halfway through and adding more water if necessary.

Add the lime juice, parsley and coriander and stir carefully. Transfer the meatballs and sauce to a serving plate and serve immediately.

Escondidinho de Salmon Com Espinafre

SPINACH AND SALMON SHEPHERD'S PIE

My interest in cooking began when I was eight years old. By 12, I had already cut out and saved newspaper and magazines recipes by the hundreds. As I grew older, my preoccupation with cooking turned into an obsession. It took me a long time to realise that knowing how to cook was a special skill and something to proud of. No one else my age shared the joy of cooking, at least not where I was from. There was one particular magazine called *Claudia Cozinha* that was my favourite. This recipe is inspired by an article I tore out more than 20 years ago and I still find it makes a delicious dinner. Some recipes never get old.

SERVES 4–6

680g skin-on salmon fillet

Sea salt and freshly ground black pepper

5 tablespoons extra virgin olive oil

2 garlic cloves, chopped

225g fresh spinach

Freshly grated nutmeg

1 shallot, chopped

125ml crème fraîche or sour cream

1 teaspoon Dijon mustard

900g Estima or Maris Piper potatoes, peeled and quartered

125ml full-fat milk

30g unsalted butter, at room temperature

30g Parmesan cheese, freshly grated

Preheat the oven to 180°C/Gas Mark 4. Lightly coat a 18cm x 28cm baking dish with cooking spray. Cover a baking sheet with foil and spray lightly with cooking spray.

Season both sides of the salmon with salt and pepper, drizzle with 1 tablespoon of the olive oil and place skin side down on the baking sheet. Roast the salmon in the oven for 6–8 minutes until medium-rare. Remove the salmon and leave to cool a little. Flake the salmon into big chunks, place in a bowl and cover with foil. You should have approximately 400g.

Heat 2 tablespoons of the remaining olive oil in a large frying pan over a medium heat. Add the garlic and cook for about 1 minute until it just starts to turn golden. Immediately add the spinach and toss everything with a pair of tongs, turning the leaves and bringing the garlic to the surface. Cook for about 2 minutes until the spinach is wilted. Season with salt and pepper and nutmeg and add to the bowl with the salmon. Cover with foil again.

Wipe any garlic bits from the pan and add the remaining 2 tablespoons olive oil and the shallot. Cook over a low heat for about 2 minutes until just softened. Add the crème fraîche and mustard and cook until the crème fraîche is just melted (don't let it boil). Season with salt and pepper. Add to the bowl with the salmon and spinach. Fold everything together, taste and adjust the seasoning if necessary. Spread the filling in the prepared baking dish and cover lightly; set aside.

Have a potato ricer or food mill ready. Place the potatoes in a medium saucepan and fill with cold water to come 2.5cm above the potatoes. Add 1 tablespoon salt, partially cover and bring to the boil. Reduce the heat to medium and cook until the potatoes are fork-tender.

Meanwhile, heat the milk in a small saucepan. When the potatoes are done, immediately drain them into a colander and pass them through the potato ricer or food mill, at the same time adding the hot milk and the butter. Stir the mashed potato with a wooden spoon or rubber spatula and adjust the seasoning with salt. Spoon the potatoes over the salmon–spinach filling and spread evenly with an angled palette knife. Sprinkle with the cheese.

Place the dish on the prepared baking sheet and bake for about 30 minutes until the edges start to bubble and the top is lightly browned. Remove from the oven and leave to rest for 5 minutes before serving.

Ervilhas com Ovos

FRESH PEAS WITH SUNNYSIDE-UP EGGS AND SAUSAGE

If you like peas, like most Brazilians do, then this dish is for you. It highlights the vegetable in a healthy and delicious way, with the oozing egg yolks over the peas and sausage adding a satisfying touch of luxury. I have made this recipe with success many times using frozen peas, but when I get my hands on fresh peas, it's even better. In Rio I always prepare this dish with linguiça (traditional Brazilian sausage); at home in the USA, if I cannot get linguiça at a Brazilian store, I use chorizo.

SERVES 4

355g linguiça or chorizo

2 tablespoons extra virgin olive oil

½ onion, chopped

2 garlic cloves, very finely chopped

450g peas

250ml chicken stock or water

Sea salt and freshly ground black pepper

30g unsalted butter

4 medium eggs, at room temperature

2 tablespoons chopped fresh parsley

Split the sausages in half lengthways and cut into 1.25cm pieces. Heat the olive oil in a large frying pan over a medium heat. Add the sausage and cook, stirring occasionally, for about 5 minutes until all the pieces are slightly crisp. Using a slotted spoon, transfer to a bowl and cover with foil to keep moist.

Using the fat rendered from the sausage, add the onion and reduce the heat to low. Cook for about 2 minutes until softened and translucent. Add the garlic and stir. Add the peas and cook for about 2 minutes until they are warmed through. Add the chicken stock and sausage, season with salt and pepper, cover the pan and simmer for 5 minutes.

Meanwhile, heat a large, non-stick frying pan over a medium heat. Melt the butter and crack in the eggs. Season with salt and pepper and cook the eggs sunny-side up until the whites are cooked but the yolks are still soft and runny. Add the parsley to pan with the peas, slide the eggs over the peas and cook for a further minute over a low heat. Spoon a mound of peas, sausage and egg onto individual plates, scooping some of the sauce from the base of the pan on top. Serve immediately.

Carne Moída Com Ovos e Azeitona

MINCED BEEF WITH HARD-BOILED EGGS AND OLIVES

For most of my life I grew up on a tiny street located at the end corner of Leblon, called Rua Aperana. My building faced the oncoming street, and even though I didn't have a view of the beach, we had a view of the beginning of Canal at Rua Visconde de Pirajá, which leads you to other neighbourhoods including Jardim Botânico and Gávea.

My life was built around that corner of Leblon, with my after-school activities consisting of learning English twice a week at Ann Arbor English Studies, located just a few steps from Rua Aperana, then a walk to the Columbia gym centre. Back home I would always look forward to eating *carne moída com ovos e azeitona* (accompanied by rice and beans, as a good carioca) on the veranda of my apartment. More often than not, this recipe is all that I need to bring those childhood memories back.

SERVES 4

2 medium eggs

2 tablespoons extra virgin olive oil

3 garlic cloves, very finely chopped

1 small onion, chopped

3 plum tomatoes, peeled, deseeded and diced

2 teaspoons dried oregano

Sea salt and freshly ground black pepper

½ chicken stock cube (I use Knorr)

450g beef mince

Freshly grated nutmeg

60g kalamata olives, pitted and roughly chopped

4 tablespoons chopped fresh parsley

Place the eggs in a small saucepan, cover with cold water and bring to the boil. Reduce the heat to low and cook until the eggs are hard-boiled. Remove the eggs from the water and shock them in iced water. Shell them and roughly chop.

Meanwhile, heat the olive oil in a medium saucepan over a medium heat, add the garlic and cook, stirring constantly, for about 2 minutes until lightly browned. Add the onion and cook for about a further 3 minutes until softened and translucent. Add the tomatoes and oregano and season lightly with salt and pepper. Crumble the stock cube into the mixture and cook for about 2 minutes until the ingredients start to blend.

Add the mince and mix well, breaking it up to avoid big lumps, then cook for 5–8 minutes until cooked through. Season with salt and pepper and nutmeg (but don't forget about the coming saltiness of the olives). Add 125ml water, partially cover the pan and reduce the heat to low. Cook for about 25 minutes until the mince is rich with flavour (you might add another tablespoon or so of water if needed). This can be done up to 3 days ahead of time.

Just before serving, fold in the chopped eggs, olives and parsley.

Arroz de Forno

BAKED RICE WITH CHICKEN AND CHORIZO

Arroz de forno is a classic dish in any carioca's kitchen – there is always rice ready in the fridge, and we find many different recipes in which to use it. In Rio, most cooks prepare this dish with pre-cooked rice, but I prefer to use uncooked rice, for two reasons: first, it's less time-consuming; second, the aroma of cooked rice is fresher and the grain is even more fluffy, fragrant and moist. This dish is extremely flexible, and you can opt to use other kinds of meat or vegetables. Follow the proportion of rice to stock to meat and you're off to a great meal!

SERVES 4

- 3 tablespoons extra virgin olive oil
- 115g chorizo, cut into 6mm slices
- 1 boneless, skinless chicken breast, about 115g, cut into 1.25cm cubes
- Sea salt and freshly ground black pepper
- ½ small onion, finely chopped
- 2 spring onions, white and green parts, chopped
- 3 garlic cloves, very finely chopped
- 2 plum tomatoes, peeled, deseeded and diced
- 200g white basmati or jasmine rice
- 750ml chicken stock
- 115g green beans, cooked and diced

Preheat the oven to 180°C/Gas Mark 4 and lightly coat an 18cm x 28cm baking dish with cooking spray.

Heat 1 tablespoon of the olive oil in a medium saucepan, add the chorizo and cook for about 2 minutes on each side until lightly browned. Transfer to the prepared baking dish, cover with foil and set aside.

Season the chicken with salt and pepper. Add the remaining 2 tablespoons olive oil to the pan, add the chicken and cook, stirring occasionally, for about 4 minutes until just cooked through. Transfer to the same baking dish, spreading evenly over the chorizo, and cover with foil again.

Still using the same pan and any remaining oil left on the base (add a little more if necessary), add the onion and spring onions, scraping the browned bits from the base of the pan. Add the garlic and cook for a further minute. Add the tomatoes and cook, stirring with a wooden spoon, for about 2 minutes until the vegetables are softened.

Add the rice and stir quickly to coat well. Add the stock and bring to the boil. Season with salt and pepper. Uncover the chicken and chorizo. Carefully ladle everything from the pan into the baking dish. Mix in the green beans and slowly stir with a wooden spoon, distributing the ingredients evenly into the rice. Bake, uncovered, for about 25 minutes until the rice is cooked.

Remove from the oven and serve immediately.

Filé de Frango Enrolado no Minas Temperado

ROLLED CHICKEN BREAST WITH MINAS CHEESE AND FRESH HERBS IN MARINARA SAUCE

Chicken and Catupiry cheese are paired all over Rio (and all inside this book too!). Chicken and Minas cheese, on the other hand, not too often. Yet Minas cheese provides a lovely texture within the rolled chicken in this recipe. There is some work and technique involved, especially when it comes to butterflying and tying the chicken. I must confess I have never mastered the butcher's way of using kitchen string, and the two ends of the chicken breast always suffer from my poor tying skills. Even though I don't make the most perfect embroidery, once cooked and simmered in tomato sauce, the chicken looks gorgeous and always tastes sublime. If you can't find Minas cheese, you can use feta or ricotta salata instead.

SERVES 2–4

10g fresh parsley, chopped

10g fresh coriander, chopped

1 tablespoon chopped fresh thyme

30g Parmesan cheese, freshly grated

35g Minas cheese, or feta cheese or ricotta salata, grated or crumbled

1 garlic clove, very finely chopped

6 tablespoons extra virgin olive oil

Sea salt and freshly ground black pepper

2 boneless, skinless chicken breasts (680g)

35g dried breadcrumbs

625ml ready-made marinara pasta sauce

Combine the herbs, cheeses, garlic and 4 tablespoons of the olive oil in a medium bowl. Season with salt and pepper and mix together with a rubber spatula.

Cut each chicken breast vertically in half on a chopping board without cutting right through, then open out like a book. Place between a sheet of clingfilm and pound thinly and evenly, trying not to let the flesh tear. Season with salt and pepper on both sides. Divide the filling between the chicken breasts and spread across the entire open surface. Roll up the chicken and tie with kitchen string (alternatively, you can secure it with skewers).

Pour the breadcrumbs on a plate and roll the chicken breasts through them to coat lightly.

Heat the remaining 2 tablespoons olive oil in a medium frying pan over a medium heat. Add the chicken breasts and cook, turning often, for 6–8 minutes until lightly browned all over.

Add the marinara sauce to the pan and bring to a simmer, scraping up the browned bits from the base of the pan with a wooden spoon. Simmer, turning occasionally, until the breasts are tender but firm.

Untie the chicken and cut into 6mm slices. Arrange on a plate and serve with the marinara sauce on the side.

Carne Assada de Panela com Batatas Douradas

BRAZILIAN-STYLE POT ROAST

I learned how to make this recipe from a friend's mother, Dona Angelina Aparecida Masieiro Braz, who is an awesome cook. It's healthy comfort food, a classic meat and potatoes dish. Dona Angelina uses water to cook the roast in, relying on the browning of the meat to give the sauce its full flavour and gorgeous mahogany colour. I couldn't escape my formal culinary background, so I made the recipe with stock, resulting in a richer sauce. Chicken stock is what I have most frequently in my kitchen, so that's what I usually use, but any flavourful stock will work. (When I have leftover veal or beef bones, I don't let them go to waste and save them for stock – call me a stock maniac!). The potatoes become golden brown and tender as they cook in the sauce. You can also use beef brisket instead of chuck and blade. It is important to keep the pressure cooker on a low heat at all times. If you don't have a pressure cooker, you can use a large saucepan or flameproof casserole dish; add 1½–2 hours to the cooking time.

SERVES 4-6

1.4kg prime beef chuck and blade joint

6 garlic cloves, grated

Sea salt and freshly ground black pepper

2 tablespoons extra virgin olive oil

3 tablespoons vegetable oil

6 garlic cloves, sliced

1 litre chicken, beef or veal stock or water

680g Chalorlotte potatoes, peeled

SPECIAL EQUIPMENT:
pressure cooker

Rub the joint with the grated garlic, season with salt and pepper and drizzle with the olive oil. Place the meat in a bowl, cover with clingfilm and refrigerate for at least 4 hours or preferably overnight. Bring the meat to room temperature 30 minutes before cooking.

Heat the vegetable oil in a pressure cooker over a medium heat. Add the beef and sear, turning frequently, for 8–10 minutes until lightly browned on all sides.

Reduce the heat to low, scatter the sliced garlic around the meat and cook until it is just golden brown, scraping the base of the pan occasionally. Don't go away; the garlic can turn from light golden to bitter dark very fast. Add the stock, cover the pressure cooker, lock the lid and cook at low pressure for about 1½ hours, checking every 30 minutes and turning the meat. Each time you check, make sure you lower the pressure from the pan first.

When the meat is done (it will shrink by almost one third), transfer to a bowl and immediately cover with foil. You should have a very dark sauce and the garlic will have seemed to disappear as it mingles with the meat juices.

Spread the potatoes evenly across the pan and cover them halfway with sauce. Cook the potatoes over a low heat, with the pan uncovered, for about 12 minutes, turning occasionally to brown them evenly.

Return the meat to the pan with any accumulated juices, reheat to warm through and serve.

Mousse de Chocolate Branca com Gelatina de Maracujá

WHITE CHOCOLATE MOUSSE WITH PASSION FRUIT GELÉE

Silky, sweet and tart, this recipe brings me back to when I was 15 years old, when I first developed a white chocolate mousse. I started with an American recipe that I got from Anne Willan's *Look & Cook* series and tried to make it work in my Brazilian kitchen. My first few attempts were failures, but there my mania for experimentation was born. This recipe is luxurious, the white chocolate mousse interlaced with a floral passion fruit gelée. The delicate pastel colours are beautiful, and you are sure to dazzle your guests with this dessert.

SERVES 8

MOUSSE

60g white chocolate, finely chopped

2 medium eggs, separated

300ml double cream

Pinch of salt

25g sugar

PASSION FRUIT GELÉE

1 teaspoon powdered gelatine

60ml water

115g passion fruit pulp, thawed if frozen

35g sugar

SPECIAL EQUIPMENT:
8 x 175ml wine glasses

Make the mousse. Place the white chocolate in a bowl and set aside.

Place the egg yolks in a medium bowl and whisk lightly.

Bring 180ml of the cream to the boil in a medium saucepan over a medium heat. Pour a little of the hot cream into the yolks and whisk well, then pour in the remaining cream and whisk again. Pour the mixture into the saucepan and cook over a low heat until it coats the back of a spoon. Immediately strain the mixture through a fine sieve directly over the white chocolate and mix with a rubber spatula until well blended. Leave to cool for 10–15 minutes until room temperature.

Whip the remaining 120ml cream in the bowl of an electric mixer fitted with the whisk attachment on medium speed. Clean the mixer bowl and whisk attachment.

Combine the egg whites with a pinch of salt in the cleaned bowl of the mixer fitted with the whisk attachment and, starting at low speed, whisk until they start foaming, then increase the speed until peaks form. Gradually add the sugar, turn the speed to medium-high and whisk until glossy peaks forms. Using a large spatula, fold the whipped cream into the white chocolate mixture, then gently fold in the whisked egg whites.

Carefully divide the mousse between the wine glasses with a small ladle or a tablespoon. Fill each glass a little above halfway, leaving space for the gelée. Refrigerate for at least 4 hours, preferably overnight.

Make the gelée. Dissolve the gelatine in the water in a small bowl. Stir and leave to stand for about 2 minutes until softened.

Heat the passion fruit pulp and sugar in a small saucepan over a low heat, whisking frequently to dissolve the sugar. Add the gelatine mixture and whisk well. Do not let it boil, otherwise the gelée will taste like gelatine.

Strain through a fine sieve into a measuring jug. Leave to cool for 15–20 minutes until room temperature, then pour into the wine glasses over the mousse. (If you leave it to stand too long, the gelée will start to harden and it won't pour as well, but it shouldn't be too hot or it will melt the white mousse.) Transfer the glasses to the fridge and chill for at least 2 hours until the gelée is set. Remove the wine glasses from the fridge about 20 minutes before serving.

Arroz Docea

BRAZILIAN RICE PUDDING

Growing up, there was always a batch of rice pudding in the fridge. Rather than eating it for dessert, I'd always stop by the kitchen after school and nosh on a bowlful for a little something sweet. As you cook this pudding, the mixture will seem a little soupy, but the beauty of this recipe is that the pudding thickens to a perfect consistency after chilling overnight. In Rio we use ordinary long-grain white rice, but I like to use Arborio rice, yielding a starchier and fatter grain of rice. You can also use white basmati or jasmine rice.

SERVES 6–8

2 x 7.5cm cinnamon sticks

1 litre full-fat milk

100g Arborio rice

30g sugar

397g can sweetened condensed milk

2 medium egg yolks

Ground cinnamon, to decorate

Smack the cinnamon sticks on a chopping board with the flat side of a chef's knife to break them up lightly.

Combine 750ml of the milk, the rice, sugar and cinnamon sticks in a large saucepan. Bring to the boil, then reduce the heat and simmer, uncovered, stirring occasionally with a wooden spoon and making the rice doesn't stick to the base of the pan, for about 20 minutes until the rice is cooked through. Remove from the heat.

Combine the condensed milk and the remaining 250ml milk in a separate saucepan.

Whisk the egg yolks in a medium bowl. Pour in a little of the condensed milk mixture to temper, whisk well, then return everything to the saucepan. Cook over a low heat, stirring slowly and constantly with a wooden spoon, for about 5 minutes until the mixture just begins to boil. Combine the mixtures from the 2 pans and cook, stirring constantly, for a further 5 minutes without letting it come to the boil.

Transfer the rice pudding to a bowl. You'll be tempted to taste it now; if you do, the rice will seem slightly sweet and too loose. Cover and refrigerate for at least 6 hours, preferably overnight. The cinnamon sticks will continue to flavour the pudding, so remove them only just before serving.

Pour the pudding into a serving bowl or divide it between individual bowls, lightly sprinkle ground cinnamon on top and serve cold.

Bolo da Benza
BENZA'S ALMOND CAKE

Although my name – Leticia – might be difficult to pronounce in English, Leticia is a very popular name in Portuguese (as well as in Spanish, French and Italian). In my high school there were several Leticias, and in my classroom alone there were three of us. To make things easier, our classmates decided to nickname us all by our last name (although between us Leticias we called ourselves Lê). My maiden name is Leticia Moreinos Benzaquen, and so, around the sweet age of 12, I became Benza. To this day, I have friends in Rio to whom I will always be Benza.

I love reuniting with friends in Rio and cooking dinner for them. Not too long ago, I invited some girlfriends over and served this almond cake, a version of a recipe I got from my dear friend and food writer David Leite. I remember the day David and I cooked together and photographed this cake for his website, leitesculinaria.com. I couldn't stop raving about it. Back in Rio, my friends went crazy over my adaptation of this almond cake, which they baptized as *Bolo da Benza* (Benza's Cake). Every now and then I receive an e-mail when someone makes the cake. It always comes with a little 'miss you and our dinners together', which brings me joy, tears and hunger to try new recipes with them the next time I am in Rio. Hopefully soon, my friends.

SERVES 6–8

Plain flour, for dusting

460g flaked almonds (see Tip)

260g sugar

165g unsalted butter

4 medium eggs, separated

½ teaspoon ground cinnamon

½ teaspoon vanilla extract

½ teaspoon almond extract

⅛ teaspoon salt

COOKING TIP: Don't use almond flour instead of flaked almonds. It's very easy to turn the nut mixture into paste and it might bring the cake down.

Place a shelf in the centre position of the oven and preheat the oven to 180°C/Gas Mark 4. Grease a 25cm springform cake tin with cooking spray, line the base with baking parchment, spray the baking parchment and dust with flour.

Place the almonds and 60g of the sugar in the bowl of a food processor and process until just ground (be careful not to overprocess – you don't want to release any oil from the nuts). Add the butter and pulse just until well incorporated (again, don't overmix).

Whisk the egg yolks and 100g of the remaining sugar in the bowl of an electric mixer fitted with the paddle attachment for 6–8 minutes until pale and thick. Add the cinnamon and vanilla and almond extracts and whisk again. Transfer the mixture to a separate bowl and set aside. Clean the mixer bowl.

Whisk the egg whites with the salt in the cleaned bowl of the mixer fitted with the whisk attachment. When they start to rise, slowly add the remaining 100g sugar and beat until soft peaks form.

Add one third of the egg whites and incorporate into the batter, then add the remaining whites, making sure the batter remains light and fluffy.

Pour the batter into the prepared tin and smooth the top with an angled palette knife. Bake the cake for 40–45 minutes until golden brown and it shrinks away from the sides of the tin. The centre will collapse a little, and that's normal. Transfer to a wire rack and leave to rest for 10 minutes before unmoulding, then leave to cool completely before serving.

GLOSSARY

Botequim

A *botequim* carries a lot of meaning for a carioca. Also called *boteco* or *bar*, the word comes from the Portuguese *botica* and from the Spanish *bodega*, referring to a place where food and drink are sold. In Rio (and in all of Brazil), the word *botequim* came to be a type of restaurant where people gather to drink and talk without much sense of time, after work or after the beach, with a certain party feeling. Recently *botequims* have been joined by more upscale cousins, a little newer and a littler cleaner, so cariocas created slang words; *pé-sujo* and *pé-limpo* ('dirty feet' and 'clean feet') as a way to distinguish between the types of *botequims*.

Carioca

A person born in Rio de Janeiro. The word comes from the Native Indian *tupi* and translates to 'white men.'

Cachaça

Cachaça is a distilled beverage from Brazil, as important to the country as vodka is to Russia and tequila is to Mexico. Essentially, it is an *aguardente*: a spirit distilled from fruits or vegetables, in this case, the juices of the sugar cane. Cachaça is distinct from rum, though, which is made from molasses, not cane juice.

Catupiry cheese

Catupiry is a Brazilian cream cheese made from fresh cow's milk, yeast, double cream, soured cream, and salt. It was first developed in 1911 by Mario Silvestrini, an immigrant from Ravenna, Italy, who opened a tiny little store in Minas Gerais with his sister, Isaira. Since 1949, however, the cheese has been manufactured in Bebedouro, in the region of São Paulo. Burnished gold in colour, catupiry has a dense, creamy texture, is slightly sweet and remains a key ingredient in classic Brazilian dishes. There are other types of cream cheese in Brazil, though we refer to them as *requeijão*, which has a thinner consistency. The name *catupiry* comes from the Native Indian *tupi-guarani* language; it means 'excellent.'

Azeite de dendê (dendê oil)

This oil is the mainstay of Bahian cuisine, and is the product extracted from the dendê palm tree, which was brought to Brazil by African slaves, back in the seventeenth century. The dendê palm tree is one of the most oleaginous in the world, producing more oil than soya beans, peanuts or coconut. The fruit and the stone are used in two different ways. The dendê oil used in cooking is extracted from the fruit pulp; first it is cooked in steam, then it is dried completely in the sun. The fruit is then crushed to release its bright orange-red oil.
The stone is also used to extract oil of a different kind, with a transparent color, mostly used for cosmetics for its similarity to cocoa butter. Often sediment forms on the bottom of a dendê oil bottle. To liquify, simply place the bottle in a bowl with warm water and let it sit for 20 minutes.

Doce de leite (dulce de leche)

This is truly a Latin ingredient produced and used all over South America. In Brazil, the state of Minas Gerais is dairy country and the biggest producer of the best dulce de leche. Essentially, dulce de leche is milk and sugar cooked slowly until it reaches the consistency of a caramelised paste. In Brazil we eat dulce de leche in all kinds of consistencies: as a candy, as a soft paste, hard paste, more sweet, less sweet, even diet. For all of the recipes in this book, I used tinned Nestlé dulce de leche.

Carne seca (jerk meat)

Carne seca is a huge part of Brazilian cooking. In Portuguese we also call it *carne de sol*, referring to salt-cured and sun-dried meat. Most jerk meats come from a lean cut, such as beef silverside, because too much marbled fat (which gives that buttery richness we want in our cooked meats) makes the dried meat too tough. Most pieces of jerk meat are cut against the grain to make them tender rather than leathery. The processes of making jerk beef vary greatly, from salting to brining, smoking in hickory or oak, or not smoking at all. Flavouring can be introduced with a dry rub, a paste, or a marinade. Drying can take place in commercial ovens, dehydrators, or naturally. The Brazilian method is less elaborate. While many of the ingredients found in this country are comparable to those found in Brazil, jerk meat is the exception, so it might taste a little different from the one eaten in Brazil. Most Brazilian stores in the UK carry a ready-made version of prepared *carne seca* that I use in some of the recipes in this book.

Linguiça

Linguiça is a type of sausage from Portugal that was brought to Brazil during colonial times. Today *linguiça* is the most adored sausage in Brazil, served in *churrascarias* (our barbecue restaurants) as hors d'oeuvres and in dishes such as *feijoada*, *farofa*, soups, and grills. The robust sausage is made from cured pork meat and flavoured with onion, garlic, and seasonings. When cooking *linguiça*, never poke the link; you don't want any fat to escape, as this is what makes the *linguiça* so moist and tender. If you can't find it, you can use chorizo or fresh sausage instead.

Manioc (tapioca) starch

Manioc starch (*povilho doce*) and sour manioc starch (*povilho azedo*) are both extracted from yucca (aka manioc or cassava). To obtain the starch, the vegetable is finely grated, mixed with water, and strained over a thick layer of cheesecloth or a fine sieve. The wet pulp is left to rest in a bucket for a day to allow the starch to sink to the bottom and completely separate from the water which, by that time, has turned yellow. To make the sour manioc starch (*povilho azedo*), this first step is prolonged for at least 15 days, until the starch is fermented under water.

This yellow water is then discarded and the process is repeated – the starch accumulated at the bottom of the bucket is scraped, mixed again with new water, sieved again through the cheesecloth, and placed in a bucket to sit for another day.

This time around, the water will be clearer and the starch accumulated on the bottom will be snow white. The water is again discarded, the starch is scraped and spread onto flat sheet pans to dry. Finally, the starch is sieved to ensure a very fine consistency.

Povilho doce (manioc starch or sweet manioc starch)

Goya calls it Tapioca Starch, but Bob's Red Mill calls it Tapioca Flour, and I call it manioc starch in this book.

Povilho azedo (sour or fermented manioc starch)

No UK brand makes the Brazilian equivalent of sour manioc starch (at least not yet), so when a recipe calls for this ingredient, do not substitute for a UK brand. I recommend Yoki or Gloriasul brands.

Farinha de mandioca (manioc flour)

Although this flour is also extracted from the yucca vegetable, the process is completely different from making starch. Here, the yucca vegetable is not washed but ground, then squeezed in a cloth to eliminate any vegetable juices, sieved, and lightly toasted. Think of it as breadcrumbs. *Farinha de mendioca* is used to make another important staple of Brazilian cuisine: farofa.

Minas cheese

Minas cheese is to Brazil what feta is to Greece, or what mozzarella is to Italy. The taste is also a cross between feta, ricotta, and mozzarella. Brazilians eat Minas cheese throughout the country, but Mineiros (people born in Minas Gerais) are really proud to have created it in their state of Minas Gerais, hence the name. Minas cheese, made from cow's milk, is white, fresh and firm. Like other fresh white cheeses, Minas has a way of complementing other flavours without masking them, and it definitely deserves more attention on its own. It is mostly consumed fresh, but the cheese can also be ripened to various degrees: *fresco* (fresh), *meia-cura* (semi-ripened), and *curado* (ripened).

Bacalhau salgado (salt cod)

Salt cod arrived on the Brazilian table through our colonisers, and today Brazil is the biggest consumer of salt cod followed by Portugal, Spain, and Italy. Brazil, however, is not a producer – all salt cod is imported from Norway and Portugal. Brazilians rarely eat fresh cod as it's just not available to us. Once reconstituted, salt cod presents a flaky flesh that is absolutely delicious. The best species of cod for salting is the Atlantic cod, *Gadus morhua*. When using salt cod, it's very important to de-salt it properly: Use a big plastic container as the volume of water has to be at least 10 times bigger than the weight of the cod. I also like to use a rack or colander so the cod is floating completely in the water. Try to find salt cod that has thick flesh.

Yucca

This tuber vegetable also goes by the names *manioc* or *cassava*. Earthier tasting than a potato and richer in starch, this vegetable is one of the foundations of Brazilian cooking. It comes from a perennial shrub with origins in the Amazon. The plant's long roots grow in clusters and are covered in a thick, shiny brown skin, and a thick white layer. When cut off, the outer layers reveal a snow white, firm interior with grey or purple veins. The centre of the vegetable also carries a woody fibre that is not pleasant to eat, but is easy to remove. Riper yuccas usually contain less fibre in their centres. Generally speaking, the thicker the yucca, the riper it is. There are so many derivatives of this one vegetable: toasted flour, flakes, starches, juices. Even the skin and leaves are used in some parts of Brazil. For home use, yucca is mostly boiled or fried and becomes very creamy with a mellow taste. When buying yucca, try to look for an even-coloured vegetable with slightly waxy brown skin and no soft or mouldy spots. Many of the yuccas sold in the UK are coated with a thin layer of wax to help extend shelf life.

RIO DE JANEIRO

N

Barra da Tijuca

Christ the Reedeemer

São Conrado

Jardim Botânico

GÁVEA

Lagoa

Leblon

IPANEMA

Copacabana

ITAIPAVA

TERESÓPOLIS

PETRÓPOLIS

BÚZIOS

PARATY

RIO

N

Ponte Rio Niteroi
NITEROI
CENTRO
SANTA TERESA
LAPA
Laranjeiras
GLÓRIA
COSME VELHO
FLAMENGO
Botafago
SUGARLOAF MOUNTAIN
LEME

INDEX

D

E

F

Q

R

S

T

V

W

Y

ACKNOWLEDGEMENTS

This book is really special to me, not only because it's a tribute to my hometown of Rio de Janeiro, but also because it kept me in two places at once: Rio and Connecticut. I am equally grateful to both, where most of my life takes place.

I grew up and became obsessed with food in Rio, but it was in Connecticut that I built my personal and professional life, thanks to the people who believed in my work.

It all started with Joy Tutela—and I am forever grateful for your guidance and continuous support. I am also grateful for the team at Westport Entertainment, Bill Stankey, Tyler Delaney, and Mary Lalli for believing in my dreams and my work.

This is my second book with Kyle Books and I can't thank them enough for that. Thank you, Anja Schmidt, for being a great editor; working with you makes me a better author. Thank you, Kate Sears, for the beautiful photos, Paul Grimes for making Rio's food look as beautiful as the city, and PJ Mehaffey for all the beautiful props. Thank you, Julie Grey and Sara Mae Danish, for testing my recipes.

No Rio de Janeiro, obrigada a todos aqueles que abriram suas portas para mim e diviram suas histórias, segredos, e receitas. Meus jantares são deliciosos por causa disso e sem vocês, este livro não seria o mesmo.

Bemdita foi a hora em que conheci o fotógrafo carioca Ricardo Mattos *em NY. É uma honra ter fotos suas da nossa cidade maravilhosa.*

Obrigada a todos os meus amigos no Rio, especialmente Tatiana El-Mann Cohe*n que além de grande amiga, foi uma ótima guia organizando viagens divertidas com nossas crianaças.*

Obrigada ao meu analista José Alberto Zusman.

Obrigada ao meu irmão Jimmy Benzaquem, *sua esposa* Fernanda, *e meus sobrinhos, Nicolas e Valentina, por estarem sempre do meu lado.*

Obrigada aos meus pais por amenizar a dor de morar longe da familia, e por recortar artigos de jornais e revistas que serviram como inspiracao para esse livro. Essas palavras são poucas para agradecer todo o amor e tudo o que vocês fazem por mim e por minha familia.

Todos os esforcos foram realizados no sentido de obter as autorizacoes das pessoas retratadas nas fotos originais do arquivo pessoal da Autora. No entanto, apesar do evidente consentimento, não conseguimos localiza-las. Razão pela qual estão reservados os direitos de imagem para atender eventuais futuras reivindicaçoes.

Thank you to the Ribacks for being a loving family and for your constant support. Thank you to all of my friends for being part of my life and sharing many meals together. Thank you also to Patti Billone.

To my handsome husband Dean, thank you for sharing your life with me and for your infinite love.

Aos meus filhos, Thomas *e* Bianca, *vocês são o ar que respiro, o sol e a lua do meu céu.*

Obrigada a minha cidade maravilhosa, Rio de Janeiro, que continua muito lindo! É uma honra dedicar este livro a você!

And finally, I want to thank everyone who bought my first cookbook and stayed in touch over the years, sending pictures, comments, and always eager to cook more Brazilian food.